Divided Berlin

DIVIDED
BERLIN

The
Anatomy
of Soviet
Political Blackmail

HANS SPEIER
The RAND Corporation

FREDERICK A. PRAEGER, *Publisher*
New York

BOOKS THAT MATTER

Published in the United States of America in 1961
by Frederick A. Praeger, Inc., Publisher
64 University Place, New York 3, N. Y.

All Rights Reserved

© 1960, 1961 by The RAND Corporation

Library of Congress Catalog Card Number: 61-17509

Printed in the United States of America

This book is Number 97 in the series of
Praeger Publications in Russian History and World Communism.

Preface

A FIRST VERSION of this study was finished before the abortive summit conference in Paris in May, 1960. Reproduced by The RAND Corporation under the title *The Soviet Threat to Berlin,* the study served as the basis of a lecture I gave at the Princeton University Conference on "Germany: Problems and Prospects," on March 16, 1960. The text was revised and expanded in June and July, 1961, resulting in the present version. It contains six new chapters, in addition to revisions in the original text, to provide an account of Communist moves and Western countermoves to the end of July, 1961.

Since the beginning of the Berlin crisis in November, 1958, I have often discussed its political implications with several of my friends and colleagues at RAND. I owe much to these discussions and am particularly indebted to W. Phillips Davison and Leon Gouré, who went with me to Europe early in 1959 to study various aspects of the conflict. On this and a subsequent visit, I talked with many Germans of various political persuasions about the Communist threat. Although this book is based primarily on a study of events and diplomatic exchanges, it could not have been written without the benefit of these personal contacts, particularly in Berlin and Bonn.

Herbert Goldhamer and Arnold Horelick read large parts of the study in draft form. I am very grateful to both of them for their critical comments and valuable suggestions.

H. S.

Santa Monica, California
August 1, 1961

Contents

	Preface	v
1	The Setting	3
2	A Demilitarized Free City	9
3	A Separate Peace Treaty	15
4	Abnormality	24
5	Blackmail	28
6	Ultimatum?	31
7	The Risks	38
8	Geneva	49
9	Camp David: New Tactic	57
10	Berlin and Bonn	69
11	Status Quo?	79
12	The U-2 Incident and the Paris Conference	99
13	Cold War by Proxy	113

14 *Vienna: The New Offensive*   125
15 *The Counterattack*   145
16 *Conclusions*   160
    Postscript   173
    Notes   186

Divided Berlin

1

The Setting

THE CURRENT CRISIS over Berlin is rooted in the fact that after Hitler's downfall the victors in World War II were unable to agree on the restoration of Germany as a state. Earlier plans of partitioning notwithstanding, the division of the country into zones of occupation was intended as a provisional measure. The zonal occupation authorities were not superseded by a new German government, because the Soviet Union on the one hand and the Western powers on the other represented different political, economic, and social systems, and each side proceeded to restore Germany in the image of its own world.[1] Agreement on the political liquidation of the war was possible only among the Western capitalist democracies, but not between them and the

Soviet Union. In consequence, the Federal Republic of Germany emerged in the Western part of the country and the Communist puppet regime of the so-called German Democratic Republic in the Soviet Zone. The reunification of Germany remained one of the issues dividing the East and the West.

The Soviet Zone, or the German Democratic Republic, with 17 million people, which is less than one-third of the population of the Federal Republic, has an area less than half the size of West Germany. More than one-third of the territory of the German Democratic Republic had been conquered at the end of the war by the armies of the Western powers but was assigned by inter-Allied agreement to the Soviet Union as part of its zone of occupation. In this way, such cities as Chemnitz, Erfurt, Leipzig, Halle, Dessau, and Magdeburg became part of the Communist empire.

Greater Berlin lies in the midst of the Soviet Zone. The distance from the city to the part of the former German Reich that is now administered by Poland is shorter than the span of 110 miles from Berlin to the West German border. Despite Communist claims to the contrary, Greater Berlin is not part of the Soviet Zone. Since Berlin was the former capital of Germany, the enemies of Nazi Germany agreed during the war to occupy and rule the city jointly.[2] Accordingly, the city was divided into four sectors, corresponding to the division of the country into four zones. Each of the

4

four powers stationed military contingents in its sector of the city. The Soviet Union violated the four-power status of Berlin when it established the government of the German Democratic Republic in East Berlin.

Access to Berlin is not a problem to the Soviet forces since they occupy the zone that surrounds the divided city on all sides. The rights of access of the Western powers are based on conquest and agreements with Soviet authorities. At the time of the Communist blockade of Berlin in 1948–49, West Berlin was cut off from West Germany, but did not succumb, because the Western allies used the three military air corridors running from West Germany to Berlin for the airlift that saved the city. It was the most massive use of air power for peaceful, political, and humanitarian purposes in history, and it was spectacularly successful. West Berlin remained free.[3]

In Berlin, the line that separates the free world from the area of Communist rule runs through the streets of the city. Liberty, prosperity, and a Western style of life prevail in West Berlin, with its modern cosmopolitan spirit, its humor, and its skepticism, while East Berlin has become a Communist settlement that is drab, noisy with propaganda, unfree, and unsafe for freedom-loving men.

About 11,500 Western occupation forces are stationed in Berlin. The more than 2 million West Berliners regard them as protectors of their right to live and work in freedom. The West Berliners are jealously proud of their liberty. With Communism at their door, they do not take freedom for granted. During elections, more than 90 per cent of the eligible voters go to the polls. The last elections were held in December, 1958, just after Khrushchev had issued his ultimatum to the Western powers proposing to deprive West Berlin of its present freedom by turning it into a "demilitarized Free City." Only 1.9 per cent of the West Berliners cast their votes for the Communist candidates. The West Berliners are politically disciplined, alert, and courageous. At times, they look upon the West Germans with the feeling that soldiers under enemy fire at the front have for their comrades in the rear.

The West Berliners remember the airlift. They remember many Communist provocations, including cases when Germans were seized by Communist agents in West Berlin and abducted across the street into East Berlin to disappear forever.[4] They know that Walter Ulbricht, now First Secretary of the Central Committee of the communist Socialist Unity Party (SED) in the Soviet Zone, abroad at the time of the Hitler–Stalin pact, called upon German workers to fight for the Nazis against the British, in support of the then-prevailing Soviet pro-Nazi policy. They remember the year 1953, when uprisings in East Berlin and various cities in the Soviet Zone were ruthlessly suppressed by Soviet forces. They know that the living

6

conditions in East Berlin and in the Soviet Zone make a farce of Communist propaganda about the accomplishments of Khrushchev's puppet regime. They know that many thousands of Germans are imprisoned for political reasons in the German Democratic Republic.

Above all, they know of the refugees, men and women of all ages, who fled to West Berlin and went from that city by air to West Germany. Air transport from West Berlin to West Germany was the only means that German refugees from the Soviet Zone—and West Berliners—could use to get out of the city without passing the control points that are manned by functionaries of the Soviet Zone regime.

The stream of refugees from the Soviet Zone to West Germany had been a drain on the manpower resources of the Soviet Zone and had delayed its economic progress. Despite the fact that a certain percentage of the refugees returned to the Soviet Zone, the immigration of Germans toward the West since 1945 was living testimony to the way in which the Germans view the political and economic conditions of the regime under which they are forced to live. From 1949 to the end of 1960, more than 2.5 million refugees applied for permission to reside in the Federal Republic.[5]

Until August 13, 85 per cent of all refugees sought a haven in West Berlin, since Ulbricht has taken ruthless measures to prevent any crossings of the zonal border. Since May, 1952, the line of demarcation separating the Soviet Zone of Germany from the Federal Republic has become an elaborate system of barbed-wire fences, guard towers, "death zones," trenches, and plowed strips of land—all to prevent border crossings.[6]

On July 25, 1961, President Kennedy said that West Berlin "has many roles":

> It is more than a showcase of liberty, a symbol, an isle of freedom in a Communist sea. It is even more than a link with the free world, a beacon of hope behind the Iron Curtain, an escape hatch for refugees.
>
> West Berlin is all of that. But above all it has now become—as never before—the great testing place of Western courage and will, a focal point where our solemn commitments and Soviet ambitions now meet in basic confrontation.[7]

2

A Demilitarized Free City

AFTER SOME PRELIMINARY storm signals in September and October, 1958, and following Khrushchev's speech of November 10, the Soviet Government presented diplomatic notes to the three Western powers and the Federal Republic on November 27, 1958, proposing a radical change in the four-power status of Berlin.[1] The Soviet Government declared that it regarded the international agreements of September 12, 1944, and May 1, 1945, concerning the zones of occupation in Germany and the administration of Greater Berlin as no longer having any validity. After speaking of "the unlawful occupation of West Berlin" and of "the severe abuse of the occupation rights" by the Western powers for the purpose of damaging the Soviet Union, the German

9

Democratic Republic, and the other socialist countries, the Soviet Government proposed the "demilitarization" of West Berlin, that is, the withdrawal of all military forces from the city, and the establishment of West Berlin as a "Free City." Its new status, the notes pointed out, could be guaranteed by the four powers either alone or in co-operation with the United Nations.

The Soviet Government further informed the Western powers that it had decided to take measures to bring its occupation of East Berlin to an end, in order to serve the cause of peace and to normalize the situation in Berlin in the interest of a peaceful and independent development of Germany.

The Soviet Government declared its readiness to negotiate with the Western powers about its proposal to establish a "demilitarized Free City" of West Berlin, but added three important stipulations. First, it intimated that the period allowed to attain four-power agreement on the Soviet proposal should be limited to six months. The Soviet Government declared that it would not change the existing procedure for military traffic of the United States, Great Britain, and France between West Germany and West Berlin for this period of six months, that is, until May 27, 1959.

Second, the Soviet Government declared that if the Russian proposal were unacceptable to the Western powers, no four-power negotiations on the status of Berlin could take place.

A Demilitarized Free City

In this case, as its third stipulation, the Soviet Government would conclude an agreement with the East German Government bestowing full sovereignty upon the latter, "on land, on water, and in the air," that is, including the approaches to Berlin.

The stipulation of the time limit was couched in ambiguous language. In one sentence, the period of six months was referred to as sufficient "to provide a sound *foundation for a solution* of the problems connected with the change of the position of Berlin"; but in another sentence it was stipulated that the period of six months ought to be used "for *reaching* a relevant *agreement*" (italics added). Similarly ambiguous were Khrushchev's immediate comments on the note. At his press conference of November 27, he announced that the Soviet Union would carry out its threat if the Western powers failed to *agree* to the Soviet proposals within six months. But at an Albanian Embassy reception in Moscow, held on the following day, he was reported—though not in the Soviet press—to have said that the Soviet Government would not act unilaterally if the Western governments agreed to *begin negotiations* within six months.[2]

Thus the Soviet note may be said to have included demands of three different kinds: a *minimum* demand that international negotiations on the future of West Berlin begin prior to May 27, 1959; *intermediate* demands that international agreement be reached by that

11

date; [3] and a *maximum* demand that West Berlin be a demilitarized Free City by May 27, 1959.

The more exacting demands were probably included in order to increase the chance that at least the lesser demands would be accepted. It appears that the use of this tactic is deliberate in Soviet diplomacy. It may be designed to confront the opponent with uncertainty as to the precise nature of Soviet intentions and to increase his willingness to meet the lesser demands. When he refuses to meet the maximum demand and is concerned over its threatening nature, attempts can be made to "appease" him by reassurances that his concern results from a misunderstanding on his part. The use of this tactic also enables the Kremlin to engage in a variety of maneuvers. For example, the Soviet Government can retreat from an advanced diplomatic position without loss of face, if a retreat appears necessary in view of alarming countermoves by the opponent. Conversely, the opponent's face can be saved more easily, should that be necessary to enable the Soviets to secure an advantage in negotiation.[4]

In the concluding paragraphs of the Soviet note of November 27, any possible attempt on the part of the Western powers not to recognize the turnover of controls from Soviet to East German authorities was associated with "methods of blackmail and reckless threats of force." In other words, the Soviet Government indicated that the German Democratic Republic would have Russian backing in refusing the Western powers the continued presence of occupation forces in West Berlin and their access to the city through and over East German territory. The Soviet Government warned that the U.S.S.R. and all member states of the Warsaw Pact would regard "every violation of the frontiers of the German Democratic Republic" as an attack on all members of the Pact and would jointly and immediately take "corresponding countermeasures." "Only madmen," the note read, "can go to the length of unleashing another world war over the preservation of privileges for occupationists in West Berlin."

Finally, the note suggested that the Soviet proposal to turn West Berlin into a "demilitarized Free City" was really a magnanimous offer, since it took account of "the present unrealistic policy" of the Western powers toward the East German Government, that is, their unwillingness to recognize the Communist regime. Basically, the note implied that the Soviet proposal was incorrect and unnatural, because "the most correct and natural way to solve the problem" of Berlin would be the unification of the divided city and the absorption of Berlin into the Communist part of Germany. Thus only through "a concession, a definite sacrifice by the German Democratic Republic" would it be possible to establish a Free City "within its territory." That gov-

13

ernment was prepared, however, to make this sacrifice for the sake of peace in Europe and in the interest of the German people as a whole.

The Soviet note brought to a head a crisis that had been adumbrated in 1948, when West Berlin withstood a Communist blockade, and less dramatically, but as it now appears more portentously, again in 1955, when the Soviet Union declared the Pankow regime to be sovereign, in the "Treaty Concerning the Relations Between the German Democratic Republic and the Union of the Soviet Republic." On the same day, November 20, Deputy Foreign Minister V. A. Zorin and East German Foreign Minister Lothar Bolz exchanged letters in which it was stated that Soviet troops would continue to exercise control over Allied traffic to West Berlin "for the time being." Subsequently, East German claims to sovereignty over the air above its territory were published as early as October, 1957.[5]

At the time that the Soviet note was published and commented on in the West, relatively little attention was paid to the fact that the Soviet Government had de-emphasized, but in no way renounced, the illegal claim to West Berlin as an integral part of the Communist German Democratic Republic. In fact, by implication the Soviets had reiterated this claim and could, at any time of their own choosing, turn it into the central issue.

3

A Separate Peace Treaty

THE WESTERN POWERS were shocked by the political aggressiveness of the Soviet Government. They pointed out that the historical account of developments during and after World War II, as contained in the notes, showed no respect for truth. They insisted that the presence of the Western powers in Berlin was based on agreements with the Soviet Union and could not be repudiated unilaterally; [1] nor were they willing to negotiate "under menace or ultimatum." [2]

The Western powers did not aggravate the crisis, however, by refusing to enter into negotiations with the Soviet Union, by alerting or redeploying their forces, or by taking other possible defensive measures of a military nature. Instead, they decided to resist the

15

Soviet assault by diplomatic means. To this end, they had to find a way of dealing with the Soviet ultimatum that would save the faces of all powers concerned, and they had to propose an agenda for discussions with the Soviet Government that would be acceptable to both sides.

Regarding the ultimatum, the Western powers pointed out that if it was the intent of the Soviet Government to urge the Western powers to conduct negotiations while threatened by unilateral Soviet actions, they could not embark upon any discussions but would have to protest in the strongest terms. On the question of the agenda, the Soviet note had left an opening for the Western powers. The Soviet proposal for "an independent solution of the Berlin problem" had been justified on the grounds, among others, that the Western powers were refusing to take part in the preparation of a peace treaty with Germany. But by the end of December, 1958, the Soviet Government had not yet replied to the Western notes of September 30, 1958, in which the Western powers had again declared their willingness to discuss the German problem in its entirety. In their answers on December 31, 1958, to the Soviet ultimatum, that fact was mentioned, and it was pointed out that "the form of government in Berlin" was "only one aspect and not the essential one" of the German problem. The Western governments said that they were ready to discuss with the Soviet Government reunification and European security "as well as the peace treaty." In this manner, by enlarging the issue, the Western powers hoped to keep the Berlin crisis within diplomatic bounds.

In persistent opposition to Soviet policy, the Western powers had always held that the formation of an all-German government on the basis of free elections—that is, reunification—would have to precede a German peace treaty. The German issue had been deadlocked, but the Soviet Union had been prevented from legalizing and fully consolidating its power reaching deep into Europe. If the Soviet notes of November 27, 1958, were meant as a prelude to a unilateral change in the status of Berlin in favor of the Soviet Union within six months, the Western replies of December 31 tried to reassert at least the existence of a deadlock. But if the Soviet notes were a device to force the West into negotiations at a summit conference on the recognition of the permanent division of Germany, the Soviet Union had improved its political position through the ultimatum of November 27. For the Western powers offered negotiations on the broader German issues. The Kremlin responded within ten days, on January 10, 1959, by proposing a high-level meeting on a peace treaty with Germany and on a series of other East-West conflicts.

The Soviet Government insisted that if the agenda was enlarged, a peace treaty with the two German governments, not reunification, ought to be the subject of four-power negotiations. The very severe draft terms of January 10, 1959, proposed for this treaty made it unmistakably clear that the Kremlin did not intend to compromise on German reunification. The Kremlin insisted, as it had done ever since 1955,[3] that unification must be left to negotiations between the two German governments and that it must take the form of a neutralized confederation in which the "social achievements" of East Germany would be preserved. The Soviet peace terms were in fact another attempt to force the West to recognize the East German Government and either to accept the Communist idea of a German confederation or to put up with the permanent division of Germany. Soon thereafter, on March 6, 1959, at the Ninth All-German Workers' Conference, a Communist meeting in Leipzig, Khrushchev declared that for the time being the Germans could live quite well without reunification; that problem would eventually be settled along Marxian lines by the class struggle.[4]

In Khrushchev's speech of November 10, 1958, and the subsequent notes of November 27, the threat to Berlin was not associated with the conclusion of a peace treaty, but on January 10, 1959, the ground was prepared for modifying the threat to Khrushchev's advantage. At this point, the threat could be presented as a consequence of Western refusal to sign a peace treaty with both German governments prior to reunification. On February 17, 1959, for the first time Khrushchev threatened to sign a separate peace treaty with the German Communist authorities in the Soviet Zone. Since then, he has repeated this threat many times. He reiterated it to President Kennedy in Vienna, early in June, 1961.

The modification of the original threat enabled Khrushchev to be deceptively conciliatory on the status of Berlin as an isolated issue, since that problem could now be attacked in the larger context of negotiations on a peace treaty with Germany. He could offer, or even hope that the Western governments would offer, an "interim solution" of the Berlin issue. In fact, this is what happened at the Foreign Ministers' Conference in Geneva.

As long as Khrushchev could point out that a peace treaty would extinguish Western occupation rights in Berlin, he did not have to repeat his original unilateral abrogation of the four-power agreements establishing these rights. He could even concede the *present legality* of Western occupation rights in Berlin as long as he remained adamantly opposed to their unlimited *continuation* in the future and maintained that the signing of a peace treaty would invalidate all obligations regarding Germany's occupation.[5] This is precisely what he has done.

The modified threat of February 17, 1959—signing a separate peace treaty—was more serious than the original one of November 28, 1958—demanding unilateral abrogation of the occupation rights in Berlin (without signing a peace treaty). The new threat included the old one, but did not carry quite so clearly the stigma that the Western powers successfully attached to the unilateral repudiation of the four-power agreement on Berlin. Furthermore, a separate peace treaty with the Pankow regime would enlist the active co-operation of various lesser powers that fought against Germany in World War II and are now in the Soviet camp. Also, the conclusion of such a treaty could possibly appear unobjectionable to neutral countries that might find fault with other ways of forcing the Western powers out of Berlin.

A final difference from the unilateral action proposed in the note of November 28 was that a separate peace treaty would deal with Germany's eastern frontiers. The Western powers failed to protest that such a unilateral settlement of the borders would violate the Yalta and Potsdam agreements, according to which the final determination of the present "line of demarcation," the Oder-Neisse Line, was to be made in the peace settlement with Germany; all four powers, of course, must participate in that settlement. But the Oder-Neisse Line has become an issue on which the Western powers are much less united than they are on their right to remain in Berlin.

In particular, General de Gaulle, while standing fast on these rights and opposing the recognition of the

Pankow regime, has often expressed the view that the present borders of Germany ought to be permanent, which comes very close to the Communist view that they *are* permanent. For example, at a press conference on March 25, 1959, De Gaulle pointed out that a unified Germany would have to accept her present borders.[6] Similar views are widespread in other NATO countries, including the United States. This does not alter the fact that the U.S. Government has not officially surrendered its right to participate along with the other major powers in the settlement of Germany's permanent borders.

Since the Moscow Conference of 1947, the Soviet Government has taken the position that the Oder-Neisse Line is not a temporary boundary but a permanent border, or, as the puppet government of the German Democratic Republic called it in the Warsaw Declaration of June, 1950, "the eternal frontier of peace." The political disunity and lassitude of the West on this issue have played into Khrushchev's hands. So has the displacement of millions of Germans from the former German territories under Polish administration, which the Western powers have tolerated. Khrushchev knows that this border issue, perhaps more than any other, evokes memories of Hitler's Germany, and he has utilized it for the purpose of associating the Federal Government with Germany's odious past.

For example, in his letter to Chancellor Adenauer on

January 28, 1960, Khrushchev pointed out not only that De Gaulle was in agreement with him on the border issue but also that the refusal of the Federal Government to recognize the existing frontiers aided and abetted those groups in West Germany that wanted to regain the eastern territories lost in World War II. He did not grant that Adenauer's position was legally sound and in basic agreement with official American policy but presented it altogether as additional proof of the Communist contention that West German rearmament threatens the security of the Communist states with an aggressive war of reconquest. Khrushchev wrote:

> Those who reject a peace treaty and raise the question of changing the borders expect to have an opportunity to settle the issue by force. This means unleashing a war. If you say that you do not want this, why do you delay in recognizing the existing borders and signing a peace treaty?
>
> In my opinion, the Federal Government's objections to a peace treaty are in large measure dictated by fear that the basis for a rearmament policy will be lost.[7]

Official American silence on the Oder-Neisse Line implies that the U.S. Government considers it unrealistic to resist a separate peace treaty with the legally valid arguments on the temporary character of the Oder-Neisse Line that can be derived from the Potsdam

Agreement. Such official silence lends force, however, to the numerous Soviet claims that the present German borders are permanent. Strictly speaking, however, these claims remain just as illegal as the Soviet claims that Western occupation rights would lapse with the conclusion of a separate peace treaty.

4

Abnormality

SINCE NOVEMBER, 1958, when the Soviet Government precipitated the current crisis over Berlin, the Communists have insisted that the political status of West Berlin is "abnormal." However, the reasons for calling the situation abnormal are various and conflicting. The Soviets, who regard the factual partitioning of Germany as normal, insist on the anomaly of Western occupation forces stationed in the midst of Communist territory sixteen years after the end of hostilities with Nazi Germany. They want to conclude peace formally with the two German governments in order to legalize the partitioning of the country and the existence of its present frontiers, especially the Oder-Neisse Line. In that event,

24

the Communist German Democratic Republic would be recognized by the West, and all occupation rights would cease. As Khrushchev pointed out in his election speech of February 24, 1959, and has since said many times, the signing of the peace treaty will invalidate all the obligations regarding Germany's occupation, both those of the Soviet Union and those of the Western powers.

Especially since his meeting with President Kennedy in Vienna, in June, 1961, Khrushchev has described the situation in Germany as well as in Berlin as abnormal.[1] He has done so in order to give greater plausibility and urgency to his demands for the conclusion of a peace treaty. In his view, such a treaty would normalize the entire situation.

The situation in Berlin and Germany is abnormal also from the Western point of view, but only because Germany has not been unified. As British Foreign Secretary Selwyn Lloyd said in Geneva:

> Mr. Gromyko has described the position in Berlin as abnormal. We have never disputed that description and have always told him that we took no pleasure in the existing situation though we regarded its continuance as being the consequence of the failure of the four powers to reunify Germany.[2]

Willy Brandt, Mayor of Berlin, made the same point more passionately in a speech in November, 1959:

The real anomaly consists after all in the fact that upon one part of Germany, or rather upon the other part of Germany, there has been imposed a regime which is rejected by the population and which must be regarded as a provocation by the German people. Or to put it more modestly: is it normal that one cannot telephone from one part of Berlin to the other? Is it normal that one cannot travel in Germany in the same way in which one can travel in Europe today? [3]

The so-called abnormality of the Berlin situation has yet another aspect, at least from the Communist point of view. The presence of Western forces in Berlin probably appears to the Soviet Government as an anachronism not only because Nazi Germany surrendered sixteen years ago, but also because Soviet military power has increased in these sixteen years relative to the power of the West. Military occupation of a territory is the strongest symbol of political predominance. In 1945, the Western occupation of West Berlin resulted from the defeat of Germany; in the meantime, it has become, in the Communist view, a Western outpost that the Soviet Union feels strong enough to challenge. To put it bluntly, if the word "abnormal" carries the connotation of "anachronistic," it refers backward, in one sense, to World War II, but forward, in another, to Soviet nuclear and missile strength in any future war.

It is not known which sense of abnormality Khrush-

chev had in mind when he said at his press conference
on November 27, 1958:

> If anyone insists on the retention of the present ab-
> normal state of affairs, he gives rise to the question
> whether he himself is normal.[4]

Soviet propaganda has repeatedly tried to exploit differences in the Western use of the word "abnormal."
For example, Khrushchev mentioned in a letter of
January 28, 1960, addressed to Adenauer, that "our
partners" in the forthcoming summit meeting in Paris
"admit that the situation in West Berlin is abnormal." [5]

5

Blackmail

IN CERTAIN WAYS, the behavior of the Soviet Government in creating the Berlin crisis followed a pattern that is familiar from Soviet conduct at the time of the Suez crisis of November, 1956, the Syrian-Turkish crisis of 1957, the Russian diplomatic and propaganda offensives against the European member states of NATO toward the end of 1957, the crisis in Lebanon, and the conflict about the islands off the shore of Communist China in 1958. In all these situations, the Soviet Union tried to make strategic and political gains by means of menacing reminders of its nuclear power and delivery capabilities, by freely uttered predictions that general war might result from the behavior of the Western powers, and by carefully veiled conditional threats of military action in defense of Communist interests.

At the time of the Lebanese crisis, President Eisenhower called the Soviet behavior "ballistic blackmail." In the Berlin crisis, the Western powers are again faced with such blackmail. Claims of Soviet military superiority, it is true, were not included in the diplomatic notes of November 27, 1958, or in the subsequent notes of January 10, 1959, which accompanied the Soviet draft of a peace treaty with Germany. Such claims were freely made, however, by authoritative Soviet spokesmen in other contexts. For example, on December 19, 1958, General M. W. Zakharov, commander of Soviet military forces in East Germany, threatened the United States with "annihilating defeat" if it were to use force against the Communists in Berlin; and he repeated a threat Khrushchev had made a week earlier that the Communist forces would strike back not only with tanks but "with more powerful weapons" in order to frustrate any Western military move to keep the access to Berlin open. Similarly, at the Twenty-first Party Congress in January, 1959, Defense Minister R. Y. Malinovsky and Khrushchev himself boasted of Soviet military strength and of superiority over the West in certain weapons, especially by claiming that the Soviet Union was now producing intercontinental ballistic missiles (ICBM's) in quantity.

Again, on June 23, 1959, in the interview he gave Averell Harriman, Khrushchev said:

> Your generals talk of maintaining your position in Berlin with force. That is bluff. If you send in tanks, they will burn and make no mistake about it. If you want war, you can have it, and remember it will be your war. Our rockets will fly automatically. . . . And his colleagues echoed like a chorus, automatically.[1]

More recently, when Khrushchev again dealt at great length with the German issue in general and the Berlin question in particular, he renewed and intensified his claims that the Soviet Union was superior to the West in strategic military power. He told the Supreme Soviet on January 14, 1960:

> We are several years ahead of other countries in the development and assembly-line production of intercontinental ballistic missiles of various types. . . .[2]

He added that the Soviet Union "would be able to literally wipe the country or countries which attack us off the face of the earth." In this speech, the most ominous one to come from the Soviet Union in the postwar era, the Soviet dictator also said that "during the first minutes" of a war, not only strategic targets would be attacked but "not a single capital, not a single major industrial or administrative center" would be spared.

6

Ultimatum?

THE BERLIN CRISIS differs in various important respects from other postwar crises in which the U.S.S.R. used military threats to obtain political gains. Let us discuss only two of them: the demand that the West abandon territory and the use of an ultimatum. In the Suez, Lebanon, and Quemoy crises, the Russians demanded that the West merely abstain from, or reverse, certain Western military moves that they deemed aggressive; but in the Berlin ultimatum, while the charge of Western aggression plays a subordinate role, the demand is for the relinquishment of territory that has been Western since 1945. Berlin's present status, which the Russians now contest, rests on an international agreement with the Soviet Union. Moreover, the presence of Western forces in West Berlin and the right of access from West Germany to West Berlin was arranged in 1945 with Soviet authorities in exchange for simultaneous withdrawal of American and British forces from Thuringia, Western Saxony, Saxony-Anhalt west of the rivers Elbe and Mulde, and from the western part of Mecklenburg. The U.S. reply of December 31, 1958, to the Soviet note on Berlin pointed out that at the time of the collapse of Hitler's empire "the Western Allies were in military possession of more than one-third of what subsequently was occupied by the Soviet authorities." [1] Indeed, this territory covered 13,500 square miles with an estimated population of 8 million. In return, the Soviet forces gave up twelve of the twenty boroughs of Berlin, or 188 square miles with 2.2 million inhabitants.[2] The extraordinary nature of the Soviet ultimatum can, perhaps, best be realized if one envisages its Western counterpart. It would consist of an ultimatum presented to the Soviet Union to withdraw its occupation forces from Thuringia and Saxony, and to transform this region of Germany into a state whose independence would be guaranteed by the four powers either alone or in co-operation with the United Nations.

On April 8, 1961, Walter C. Dowling, the U.S. Ambassador to the Federal Government, pointed out:

> The Soviet Union accepted its zone of occupation subject to Western rights of access to Berlin. If this

were not true and if the doctrine of joint and equal rights is not applicable, then, for example, the U.S. would now be free to require the Soviet Union to withdraw from that position of the Soviet Zone originally occupied by American forces and to assume control of the area.[3]

The boldness of the Soviet demands was only thinly veiled by the proposed plan also to withdraw Soviet forces from East Berlin and not to surrender West Berlin to the Communist authorities in East Germany forthwith but to turn it into a so-called "Free City." The U.S.S.R. would also welcome the alternative of stationing Soviet troops, along with Western token forces, in "free Berlin."

As for the deadline for meeting the Soviet demands on Berlin, it should be noted that in past crises the Soviet leaders have never issued their warnings to the Western powers in the form of an ultimatum. In the case of the Berlin deadline, however, they were less cautious in this regard. For reasons that I shall discuss, they were apparently confident that they could afford to challenge the West by an ambiguous ultimatum without incurring very high risks and to make gains whether the Western powers accepted or rejected their demands.

Subsequently, the Soviet leaders proved to be remarkably erratic in interpreting their ultimatum. Khrushchev and First Deputy Chairman A. I. Mikoyan extended the original time limit of six months by varying periods of days, weeks, and months. May 27, 1959, the expiration day of the original ultimatum, passed like any other day, but by that time negotiations were under way in Geneva. The uneventfulness of this day must have been disappointing, if not somewhat embarrassing, to the East German Communists, although they could boast that the Western powers were dealing with them diplomatically in Geneva. Like the Federal Republic, the East German Government participated in the Geneva Conference only in an advisory capacity, but this technicality did not prevent its functionaries from delivering aggressive speeches against the West at the conference or from efforts to efface the difference between advisory and full participation in their domestic propaganda.[4] On October 10, 1959, Otto Grotewohl, Minister President of the German Democratic Republic, declared at a rally in Berlin, "Our republic won *de facto* recognition by the Western Powers in Geneva."

On June 10, 1959, when the Western powers believed that the ultimatum had been rescinded, Gromyko in a dramatic move put forth a new time limit. He proposed that the presence of Western troops in Berlin be limited to one year, during which period the other demands of the Soviet Union would have to be met by the West. These demands were, in every important respect, the same as those stated in the original ultimatum of the previous November. A few days later, Gromyko said that it would be wrong to depict the Soviet proposals, which he did not modify at all, "as a threat, ultimatum or dictat," [5] and he extended the new one-year time limit by six months. In July, Soviet Communist Party Secretary Frol R. Kozlov, at the end of his visit to the United States, repeated Gromyko's denial that any ultimatum existed. Finally, in December, 1959, Khrushchev himself declared in Budapest:

> We are not forcing a solution of the West Berlin problem in point of time, we are setting no deadlines, issuing no ultimatums. . . .[6]

Khrushchev had come a long way in the course of one year. At his press conference of November 27, 1958, the day on which the first note on Berlin was delivered to the Western governments, he had declared:

> If the Western powers disagree with our proposals, that will not stop us. When the time [of six months] expires we will implement our proposals as stated in our documents.

Then, in December, 1959, Khrushchev not only denied the existence of any ultimatum and referred to the Western powers as "our allies," [7] but also attacked Adenauer for having served an ultimatum on the Soviet Union! [8] Thus he used a technique that is standard in Communist policy, propaganda, and diplomacy, namely that of attributing to the opponent precisely those ob-

35

jectionable actions that the Communists themselves have taken or contemplate taking.

Consider in this light the Berlin crisis as a whole. If anything, the current status of West Berlin is an example of peaceful coexistence, but the Soviet Government has created the crisis by charging that the status of West Berlin threatens Soviet security and peace. Similarly, while proposing to renounce unilaterally the four-power agreement on the occupation of Berlin, the Soviet Government charged that the presence of Western troops in Berlin was "illegal." Finally, in the Soviet note, which created the crisis by bringing pressure to bear upon the Western powers, the West was warned not to respond by resorting to "blackmail and reckless threats of force."

The Western powers, especially the United States and France, have maintained that they would not yield under the pressure of an ultimatum, and in particular that the Soviet ultimatum would preclude a meeting at the summit, which Khrushchev had sought since December, 1957.[9] The Soviet denials that a time limit for settling the Berlin issue had been set must be regarded not only as a concession to the political sensitivity and self-respect of the West, but also as a partially successful maneuver to gain some of the political advantages that the ultimatum was originally designed to attain. The ultimatum did not fail or backfire, but provided the Soviet leaders with additional bargaining power, because by belittling or withdrawing the ultimatum later, they could give the impression of reasonableness and evoke hopes for the relaxation of international tension, as if that tension had not been heightened by their own demands. By this maneuver they could perhaps also hope to foster illusions—dangerous to the West and no doubt welcome to the Communists—that the disappearance of time pressure might be regarded as the disappearance of all pressure.

After Khrushchev's visit to the United States, several leading Western statesmen—Eisenhower, Harold Macmillan, Selwyn Lloyd, and Christian Herter—addressed themselves to the question of what had changed since November 27, 1958, and all mentioned, among other things, the disappearance of the ultimatum.[10]

At the Vienna meeting in June, 1961, and especially in his June 15 report on this meeting, Khrushchev was careful not to state his renewed demands for a peace treaty in the form of an ultimatum, but he succeeded in creating the impression among the Western governments that they were under new time pressures.

7

The Risks

BEFORE THEIR POLITICAL ATTACK on Berlin, the Soviet leaders must have weighed the military—and other—risks of their venture. Generally speaking, risks are acceptable from the Soviet point of view not necessarily when they are low, but when they are controllable, that is, when circumstances permit a retreat in the event of dangerous resistance. For various reasons, the risks run by the Soviet Government in the Berlin crisis have been both low and controllable.

Paradoxically, the risks usually attending the pursuit of ambitious political aims against the interests of a powerful adversary were lowered in the case of the Berlin crisis by the nature of the Soviet threat. The immediate threats were nonviolent. The first threat—

already nearly forgotten—consisted in the warning that no negotiations could take place unless the Soviet proposal to establish West Berlin as a demilitarized Free City was accepted by the West.[1] This threat was probably made to help prevent a rejection of the Soviet minimum demand that negotiations on the future of West Berlin begin within six months. The second immediate threat was—and still is—to *withdraw force,* in other words, to withdraw Soviet occupation troops from East Berlin and transfer control of Western military traffic to and from West Berlin to East German authorities by concluding a separate peace with them.

Neither of these plans involves violence. The use of force against the Western powers has been threatened merely in retaliation against any possible future violation of East German sovereignty, and the Soviet Government has repeatedly pledged military support to such "defensive" action. If the Soviet Union concluded peace separately with the German Democratic Republic, the insistence of the Western powers on their rights to continued access to West Berlin and to the continued presence of their troops in the city would clash with East German claims of sovereignty over both the access routes to West Berlin and the territory of West Berlin itself. Ostensibly in protection of its sovereignty, the East German Government might take a variety of measures in order to compel the Western powers to relinquish their rights and to negotiate with the Communist regime; the alternatives for the West would include being the first to resort to force in an attempt to uphold these rights.

For the Communists, the situation they have created has two great advantages. First, it keeps the Western powers in uncertainty as to what the East German Government might actually do after a turnover of controls: impede, at a time of its choosing, Western military air or surface traffic? blockade West Berlin? occupy West Berlin? merely test Western tolerance for chicanery and provocation in the hope thereby of demoralizing the population of West Berlin and wrecking its economy? do nothing for the time being but continuously denounce imperialist intervention in the internal affairs of an independent state? In short, the Communists have a wide variety of choices, including avenues of tactical retreat in the event of effective Western political or military countermeasures. For example, pending a new four-power agreement on the future status of Berlin, the Soviet Government can still designate the otherwise sovereign East German Government as its agent in the exercise of control over Allied military traffic to West Berlin. Or Khrushchev can reduce pressure for a while, if the risks he incurs by his policy appear to increase. This happened, in fact, after the U-2 incident, in May, 1960.

The second Communist advantage derives from the seeming reasonableness and peacefulness of the Soviet proposals. If there were a clash of arms over the resolution of the conflict, the Communists, and, no doubt, some observers in neutral countries, would charge *the West* with aggression in defiance of the simple, peaceful measures concerning Berlin that the Soviet Government has proposed. When Khrushchev held a press conference with more than 250 Soviet and foreign correspondents on the day the Soviet ultimatum was issued, he wore a large, glistening, gold peace dove on his lapel.[2]

Moreover, the Communists would be favored both numerically and logistically in any localized encounter fought with conventional weapons. The Warsaw Pact countries possess enough power to deter a local *conventional* war in which only the Western occupation powers would fight for their presence in Berlin.

At a press conference held in France on March 25, 1960, Khrushchev admitted freely that the 11,000 troops in Berlin constituted no threat to the Soviet Union from a military point of view. He added sarcastically that it would probably be to the Communist advantage if 200,000, 300,000, or half a million soldiers were brought to West Berlin. According to Tass, this statement was greeted with laughter. And Khrushchev continued jokingly, "Then it would be easier to neutralize them in case of war." [3]

But whatever weight the Soviet leaders may have attributed initially to the risk of a local war, it must have been substantially reduced by the initial Western military reaction to the Soviet ultimatum. No military reinforcements were sent to Berlin, Western Germany, or Western Europe; no partial mobilization measures were taken by any of the three Western powers concerned; and President Eisenhower, at his press conference of March 11, 1959, clearly spoke out against the possibility of a ground war over Berlin.

Nevertheless, the Soviet Government attempted to control and arrest any Western consideration of *local* military action by disabusing the West of the idea that a military conflict over Berlin might remain localized. The Soviet public doctrine of war had long been that military conflict involving the United States and the Soviet Union was unlikely to stay limited and would probably develop into general, all-out nuclear war; that, given the far-flung interests of the two rival alliance systems—the capitalist states and the socialist states— the possibility of localizing any future war elsewhere was remote; that war in Europe would "automatically" lead to a world war; and that it would not be possible to place restrictions on the use of weapons in war. Originally, this doctrine was used in order to counter American warnings that "tactical" nuclear weapons, employed one-sidedly by the West, should be regarded as "almost conventional" in character [4] and would thus be different from the strategic use of nuclear weapons.[5] More recently, Khrushchev himself stated flatly, "War, in the present conditions, would inevitably turn into a world war." [6]

In making its prediction that limited, local war would turn into general war, the Soviet Government endeavored both to deter the outbreak of local military conflict and to shock the West into realizing the discrepancy between the fearful nature of all-out nuclear war and the seemingly narrow character of the Berlin issue.

Nevertheless, before the Soviet Government decided to challenge the Western powers in Berlin, it must have considered not only the risk of limited, local war but also the highly dangerous one of all-out nuclear war. No matter how improbable the Soviets may have judged the possibility of such a war, they could not afford to ignore the most fearful of all risks attending their diplomacy and had to attempt a reduction of that risk.

Moreover, Khrushchev was probably aware of the fact that in the event of local conventional war, the military outcome of that conflict, too, would be affected by the considerable danger of nuclear escalation. The belligerents would not necessarily be able to conduct their conventional operations according to military principles that used to be valid in the pre-nuclear age. Neither would they be able to exploit superiority in conventional weapons in the time-honored way, nor would they necessarily incur those military disadvantages attending inferiority in war in the pre-nuclear era.

At any given moment, both sides would estimate the progress of the war by gauging the magnitude of the risk of escalation prevailing at that time and not in terms of territory gained or lost or the local balance of forces. The magnitude of risk would be determined not solely by the state of the conventional ground war, but also by unforeseeable political developments that might well include negotiations while the ground war progressed and threats of resort to nuclear arms.

For many years, the Soviet public doctrine of general war had been used as a political instrument to reduce the risk that such a war would occur in consequence of Soviet foreign policy. The doctrine had sought to depreciate Western deterrence. While the West maintained that general nuclear war would mean "the end of civilization," the Soviet leaders proclaimed it to mean "the death of capitalism." They had claimed for many years that despite the grievous suffering they would sustain in a nuclear exchange, various factors—vastness of territory, dispersed location of urban centers and industry, and a relatively low population density—would render the Soviet Union less vulnerable to nuclear attack than the West European NATO countries. After August, 1957, when the Soviet Union announced that it had tested an ICBM, the Soviet Government made the same claims with specific reference to the United States. As I have mentioned, assertions regarding Western vulnerability in the arsenal of Soviet political weapons were accompanied by loud and increasingly ominous claims of Soviet strength in missiles and nuclear warheads.

More recently, public Soviet statements on the outcome of nuclear war have lost some of their frightening political buoyancy. In the October, 1960, issue of the Soviet magazine *International Affairs,* Major General N. Talensky advanced views on the nature and outcome of general nuclear war that come very close to opinions that have circulated widely in the West since 1953. Talensky stated that "nuclear war would mean that human society would be set back and that the road to Communism would be immeasurably lengthened." Previously, such views were advanced only occasionally by Communist leaders outside the U.S.S.R., such as Gomulka, Tito, and Togliatti. It is possible and, indeed, likely that Talensky's statement is an offshoot of the ideological conflict between the Communist Parties of the Soviet Union and Red China. In fact, the most irresponsible and challenging comments on the nature and outcome of nuclear war between the East and the West have come recently from Chinese rather than Russian sources.

In accordance with this modification of the Soviet view of nuclear war, Khrushchev has lately stressed the horror of such a war, rather than the certainty that Communism would survive. In terms of propaganda, he has therefore gained a better cloak for his role as the angel of peace. Although he has thereby blunted the instrument he formerly used for intimidating the West, it would not be safe to predict that he will continue to refrain from brandishing the nuclear might of the Soviet Union.

Quite the reverse is true. If the conflict becomes more intense, Khrushchev has a choice between relaxing his pressure on the West, as he did in Paris in May, 1960, or increasing it by the resumption of nuclear threats. He is most likely to increase the pressure if the political and strategic balance of forces is in his favor and the stakes are high enough to warrant incurring the remaining irreducible risks.

Khrushchev probably does not fear that the United States will attack the Soviet Union or any other Communist country. On July 28, 1959, he said in a speech at Dnepropetrovsk:

> The Party Central Committee and the Soviet Government believe . . . that the imperialists will hardly launch a war against our Motherland and the countries of socialism.

Nor is it likely that the Soviet Government ever had the bizarre intention of precipitating general war by creating the Berlin crisis. But Soviet views about limited and general war have been invoked in diplomacy and propaganda dealing with the crisis in order to impress upon the West, in Khrushchev's words, "that a fundamental shift has taken place in the balance of power between the socialist and capitalist states." [7] And in the light of this claim, Soviet behavior in the Berlin crisis has been another case of "ballistic blackmail."

From the beginning of the crisis, the Soviet Government must have been reckoning with yet another risk, namely, that of producing a Western shock reaction by overplaying its hand. The lesson of the aggression in South Korea that led to an enormous expansion of the U.S. defense budget cannot have been lost on the Kremlin. For example, Khrushchev would certainly have undercut his propaganda on coexistence, and probably would have shocked the NATO governments into an increase of their defense efforts, had he refused to hold a conference of Foreign Ministers, signed a separate peace treaty with the East German Government on May 27, 1959, and permitted incidents of violence to occur in West Berlin.

As we shall see, at the time of the abortive Paris summit conference, in May, 1960, it became clear that Khrushchev was aware of the danger of provoking an increase in American defense expenditures by his policy. Shortly after the Vienna meeting with President Kennedy, in June, 1961, the issue occupied his attention again; the increase in the American defense budget and talk about partial mobilization caused him to take countermeasures.

47

As the crisis, which he felt strong enough to create, unfolded, Khrushchev had an opportunity to observe the reactions of the West and to gauge the actual risks his policy was running. Until May, 1960, when the U-2 incident occurred, these risks did not prove to be very high. Khrushchev steered his course with adaptive skill as well as with perseverance.

8

Geneva

On February 16, 1959, the Western powers proposed a Foreign Ministers' Conference, reaffirming their intent to maintain communications with West Berlin. The next day, Khrushchev made a speech at Tula, in which he assailed this Western intent, saying Soviet troops in East Germany "are not there to play games . . . if anybody should start shooting, this would mean the beginning of war." A week later, Khrushchev declared at a press conference that a meeting of Foreign Ministers would merely increase international tension. He pressed instead for a summit meeting without a formal agenda and seemed to be probing Western weakness prior to Macmillan's visit to Moscow.

Within a few weeks, however, Khrushchev conceded

that the three Western powers had "lawful rights for the deployment of troops in Berlin as occupiers," [1] modified the ultimatum by saying that the deadline of May 27, 1959, was only an approximate date, and agreed to a Foreign Ministers' Conference to precede the summit meeting. The British press was inclined to see hopeful signs in these developments,[2] but no less than three times in March Khrushchev reiterated his threat that he would conclude a separate peace treaty with the East German Government if the Western powers failed to sign peace treaties with both German governments.

At the beginning of the Geneva Conference, Soviet policy had already been successful in various important respects. Considerable differences of opinion as to how the crisis ought to be met had come to light in the Western camp, not only between Washington, London, Paris, and Bonn, but also in the public debate in the United States. The Soviet political attack on the Federal Republic had begun to pay some dividends, inasmuch as important American and British observers shared the belief of the German Socialists that West German rearmament and Adenauer's anti-Communism rather than Soviet pressure were the causes of the international conflict.[3]

In addition, Khrushchev had moved closer toward the summit meeting, which he had so long desired to attend, and had gained an opportunity to introduce functionaries of the East German regime into the august company of diplomats representing legitimate governments. But the most important Soviet success consisted in the growing Western awareness that German reunification in freedom was disappearing from view. No matter how noble an aspiration it was, how desirable a political objective, the possibility of the peaceful attainment of reunification seemed remote. As an observer of the German situation remarked in the spring of 1959, "*All* considerations of the Western diplomats, in whatever direction they go, proceed from the tacit assumption that the division of Germany, as far as human reason can see, is final." [4]

At the meeting of Foreign Ministers in Geneva, the Western powers first presented the "package plan" of May 14, 1959, in which the reunification of Germany was linked with a solution of the Berlin issue. The plan proposed a phased procedure, insisted on the Western rights to maintain troops in Berlin, and provided for free elections in the whole of the city as a first step toward unifying the country.

The plan, of course, was rejected, because the Soviet Government held that it would perpetuate the rights of the Western powers to be in Berlin. The Soviets insisted that a peace treaty be concluded with both German governments and that reunification be left to them.

In many weeks of negotiations, the Western powers failed to get an agreement with the Soviet Union, although after the rejection of the package plan, two major attempts were made to reach a compromise—one in June, the other after recess of the conference at the end of July. These proposals, particularly the one in July, contained important concessions.

The July proposal retained some important features of the earlier proposal of June 16, including:

1. A provision for "free and unrestricted access" to West Berlin for civilian and military traffic.

2. Acceptance of the East Germans as "agents" of the Soviet Union to control this traffic. (This was suggested in recognition of the fact "that the Soviet Union wishes to cease to perform certain functions connected with access procedures," as Selwyn Lloyd had put it on June 12. Secretary of State Dulles had suggested the possibility of this concession long before the Geneva meetings began and shortly after receipt of the Soviet note of November 27, 1958.[5])

3. Maintenance of freedom of movement between East and West Berlin.

4. Establishment of a Four Power Commission in Berlin to settle disputes arising from these arrangements.

5. Curbs on (propaganda and intelligence) activities in Berlin that "might either disturb public order or seriously affect the rights and interests, or amount to interference in the internal affairs, of others."

6. A commitment of the Western allies not to station

nuclear or rocket weapons in West Berlin. (This point, characterized by Selwyn Lloyd on June 12 as "really so ludicrous as hardly to require an answer," was the only item to be found in both the Western and Soviet proposals when the conference closed.)

The last Western proposal of July 28 for an interim solution of the Berlin crisis differed in two important respects from the June 16 proposal. While the earlier proposal had stipulated that "these arrangements will continue in force until the reunification of Germany . . . unless subsequently modified by four-power agreement," the proposal of July 28 was in effect an interim agreement for five years. It stipulated that in the absence of reunification, the ministers could meet to review the situation after a five-year period at the request of any one of the four powers. Thus, the vital relationship between the settlement of the Berlin crisis and the Western policy on reunification was strained to the brink of compromise. It will be noted that the Western rights in Berlin, which the original Soviet ultimatum had contested, were not mentioned explicitly in the Western proposals of June 16 and July 28, but were merely implied.

The second major modification of the June 16 plan consisted in a new provision envisaging that the curb on propaganda activities be monitored by the United Nations. This idea had been advanced before by

Secretary Herter in a plenary session of the conference on July 16.

While the Western ministers thus sought a truce on Berlin, Gromyko's last proposal at the conference repeated Moscow's demands of June 10 and 19. In particular:

1. The reduction of the Western occupation troops to a "symbolic" size, totaling 3,000 to 4,000 men. (Acceptance of this provision would have meant a *de facto* withdrawal of the Western powers from Berlin "with all its psychological and political consequences." [6]

2. Commitment of the Western powers not to equip their troops in Berlin with atomic weapons and not to station any such weapons in Berlin.

3. A very elastic provision to prevent the use of West Berlin for "hostile propaganda" and "subversive activities against the Soviet Union, the German Democratic Republic and other socialist states." This provision was to be supervised by a Four Power Commision. (Such an arrangement would have enabled Soviet authorities to interfere in the internal affairs of West Berlin. No reciprocal arrangement for East Berlin was proposed.)

4. A unilateral Soviet guarantee of Western access to West Berlin for a period of eighteen months. (This provision was to take the place of the Western rights

in Berlin, which had been unchallenged for fourteen years.)

5. The establishment of an All-German Commission, with an equal number of members representing the Federal Republic and the German Democratic Republic, to work out resolutions on a peace treaty and on unification within a period of eighteen months.

6. If at the end of that period no agreement was reached on these two issues, "the parties to the Geneva Foreign Ministers' Conference of 1959 could take up the question of West Berlin once again." [7] (On June 10, Gromyko had not made this offer but had threatened that the Soviet Union would sign a peace treaty with East Germany after twelve months unless the All-German Commission had reached agreement on the peace treaty and unification. While he now offered that in the event of such a contingency new four-power negotiations on Berlin would be held, he refused to give any indication that the rights of the Western powers in Berlin would be the basis of such negotiations.)

All the Western powers found these proposals unacceptable. The Bonn Government did not like the last Western proposals of July 28, although it reluctantly agreed to them. The West Berliners especially were alarmed by them, and Willy Brandt warned of the pitfalls of the Western offer, particularly of points 2 and

5. In the meantime, by keeping the crisis alive, Khrushchev had enhanced his chances for both a visit to the United States and a conference at the summit. As early as March 19, 1959, he had predicted that the Foreign Ministers would not reach an agreement, and on June 23,

> While Gromyko sat silent and glum at the foot of the table [Mr. Harriman reported], Khrushchev said, "Gromyko only says what we tell him to. At the next Geneva meeting he will repeat what he has already told you. If he doesn't, we'll fire him and get someone who does." [8]

9

Camp David: New Tactic

During the geneva conference, Soviet spokesmen frequently threatened the West that if four-power agreement did not materialize, their government would conclude a separate peace treaty. Evidently, the reason the threat was made so often was to exact concessions from the Western powers.

No sooner had Khrushchev's visit to the United States been announced in June, than these threats were put in abeyance. Apparently, Khrushchev felt that such moderation was a small price to pay for improving his chances of obtaining concessions in his talks with President Eisenhower.[1] Nor was Khrushchev in any way committed not to resume his threats at any time of his choosing. As we shall see, in the last weeks prior to the Paris summit meeting, he did revert to his former style. For the time being, however, Khrushchev posed as the head of a foreign state who could talk reasonably with American business leaders and statesmen; he was ill-mannered only in his exchanges with labor leaders. He refrained from repeating his sharpest warnings, although he continued to insist that a peace treaty with "the two German states" be concluded and that reunification be left to the Germans: [2]

> Day follows night, and after war peace must come. That is why a peace treaty must be signed. With whom? With the two existing German states, because there is no united Germany.[3]

After Khrushchev's visit to the United States, the new, more moderate tone in Soviet propaganda continued, and certain other important tactical changes were introduced into Soviet policy. They can be attributed in large part to Khrushchev's talks with President Eisenhower.

The result of the talks at Camp David was summed up by Assistant Secretary of State Andrew H. Berding a few days after Khrushchev's return to the Soviet Union. Berding spoke of "one revealing index of the relationship achieved":

> This relates to the unwritten agreement that the President and the Chairman reached with regard to the

fact that the reopened negotiations on Berlin, while not to be prolonged indefinitely, would not have a fixed time limit on them. Although this language was not in the communiqué, the President and Mr. Khrushchev agreed that the President would make a statement using this language and then Mr. Khrushchev would make a statement confirming it. This procedure was faithfully carried out without delay. The agreement itself was perhaps the most important development at Camp David.[4]

In other words, Khrushchev had agreed at Camp David "to reduce pressure for a speedy settlement of the Berlin issue, at least to the extent of not making his demands in the form of an ultimatum; the heads of the Western governments would therefore not lose face by negotiating with Khrushchev in Paris." Evidently, he had also indicated that the Communists would take no unilateral measures prior to the summit meeting either by signing a separate peace treaty or by permitting the German Communists to disturb the peace in West Berlin. The President, in turn, had committed himself to visit the Soviet Union.[5] In addition, he had not fully countered Khrushchev's interpretation of the abnormality of the situation; or so it appeared to some observers after his press conference of September 28, 1959, to the extent that he failed to stress that the Soviet Government had been responsible for creating an abnormal situation in Berlin and Germany.[6] Finally, the talks at Camp David had created expectations that some interim solution for Berlin might be reached at the summit meeting.

After the Camp David discussions, the overt attack on the presence of Western troops in Berlin, epitomized in the standard demand to transform West Berlin into a "demilitarized Free City," disappeared for a while from Khrushchev's statements. Instead of that phrase, he spoke of the "Free City" at the National Press Club in Washington, D.C., September 16, 1959; in Budapest, December 1, 1959; and in Moscow, January 14, 1960.[7]

In his article in *Foreign Affairs,* in which he referred to the conclusion of a peace treaty with the two German states "as the question of questions," Khrushchev also spoke merely of the demand for "the normalization of the situation in West Berlin" and of its conversion "into a Free City." [8] Walter Ulbricht, head of the Communist Party in East Germany, used the old formula as late as November 23, 1959, in a television interview that was broadcast—to the delight of German Communists—by an American station.[9] As though he had not been advised of the change in tactic, Ulbricht said:

> We agree with the proposal of the Soviet Union that it would be useful to transform West Berlin into a demilitarized Free City. West Berlin lies in the center of the German Democratic Republic. But West Berlin has an Occupation Statute and is occupied by American, British, and French troops.[10]

The somewhat more restrained style in Soviet diplomatic and propaganda policy assumed added significance from three other tactical changes:

1. The claim that a certain relaxation of international tensions had taken place.
2. The differential treatment of Western leaders.
3. The attack on the relation between the Federal Republic of Germany and West Berlin.

The assertion that a certain relaxation of international tension had occurred, which Khrushchev managed to combine with statements of ever-increasing sharpness on Soviet missile strength, appeared at first to have been an exercise in self-congratulation on the success of the Soviet policy of coexistence in general, and on the results of the meeting at Camp David in particular. Khrushchev equated this relaxation with the alleged disappearance of the Cold War, or to put it more accurately, with the disappearance of "the former, now bankrupt, positions of strength policy, a policy of containment and deterrence, a policy of brinkmanship. . . ." [11] But his repeated assertions that international tension had diminished were almost certainly also meant to be self-fulfilling prophecies. Khrushchev apparently believed that by continually talking about relaxation he would improve his chance of reaching the agreements on Berlin and Germany with the Western powers—agreements that his threatening ultimatum had failed to achieve. Or rather, from the Communist viewpoint, the threats and the protestations of peacefulness, the ultimatum and its revocation, the missile claims and the talk about coexistence—all are thrusts toward the same unchanged political objective. Communist claims of a relaxation of tension mean that the opponent has been given an invitation to relax.

The distinction between Cold War and peaceful coexistence throws into relief the differential treatment of Western statesmen in Communist diplomacy and propaganda. Briefly, all Western statesmen whom the Russians believed might possibly agree to an understanding at the summit were treated courteously; all those who doubted the trustworthiness of the Soviet Government, and thus might call attention to the possible pitfalls of the forthcoming summit meeting, were abused and attacked; these included Adenauer and President Giovanni Gronchi, of Italy.

In examining the new Soviet tactic toward the West at the end of 1959, the *Neue Zürcher Zeitung* [12] found that the following Western statesmen were not attacked: Eisenhower, Herter, Macmillan, and Selwyn Lloyd; but there was sharp criticism of George Meany and Dean Acheson. Khrushchev's speech of January 14, 1960, contained attacks on Nelson Rockefeller, Dean Acheson, and former President Truman, who were chided for making statements on international questions "from positions which are very different from those reflected in the Soviet-American communiqué signed at Camp David." The speech was respectful toward President Eisenhower, Prime Minister Macmillan, and General de Gaulle. On April 25, 1960, shortly before the Paris meeting, Khrushchev also attacked Herter and especially Douglas Dillon.

By contrast, Chancellor Adenauer and Mayor Brandt (somewhat less frequently) were presented as the conspirators of the Cold War. Adenauer was held responsible for the differences that still existed between the Soviet Union and her Western allies and that disturbed the peace in Europe. He was said to be plotting war, and he was accused of meddling in the affairs of Berlin:

> If we still have differences and have not reached agreement on certain important questions, it is, as we believe, with adequate grounds—a result of the concessions made by the Western powers to Chancellor Adenauer. . . .[13]

In Budapest, Khrushchev asked derisively, "Mr. Chancellor, do you not see that the strength on which you rely has been lost and no longer exists?" [14] On January 14, Khrushchev again devoted a considerable portion of his speech to heaping abuse on Adenauer, accusing him of whitewashing the Nazi regime and imitating Hitler's provocative foreign policy. The campaign reached a new peak during Khrushchev's visit to France in March,

1960. The Soviet dictator used all his powers of persuasion to evoke the old French image of a powerful
Germany as the hereditary enemy threatening the
integrity of France and peace in Europe.

After Khrushchev's visit to France, the Bonn Government sent a note to Moscow protesting strongly against
the Soviet campaign of defamation. The German note
pointed out that the Federal Government did not
possess combat troops of its own under national command and had voluntarily renounced the production of
the heaviest weapons, especially that of nuclear weapons.
The note also pointed out that NATO was not designed
for *"revanchism* and militarism." The Federal Government found it "strange that this reproach is made by
a government that constantly prides itself on its strength
and that has no scruples in stating publicly time and
again that it is in a position to destroy other countries
in a few seconds in the event of war." [15]

In the cruder East German press, the "acceptable"
Western statesmen were sometimes openly cited against
the "unacceptable" ones. For example, *Neues Deutschland* wrote:

> The whole world seeks genuine relaxation. Even in
> the White House in Washington . . . it has finally been
> realized that something has to be changed in West
> Berlin, as Foreign Secretary Herter confirmed a few
> days ago. Also in Washington and London, it is recog-
> nized that the abnormal situation of a frontline city

[West Berlin] must be changed. Only in Bonn, in the City Hall of Schöneberg [the seat of the West Berlin Government], is there unwillingness to see that.[16]

Or more succinctly: "HERTER REPUDIATES BRANDT." [17]

The Communist attack on Adenauer and Brandt, and on General Hans Speidel and Defense Minister Franz Josef Strauss, followed the familiar pattern of political warfare, in which the opposing coalition is weakened by the creation of schism in its ranks. The Soviet Government tried to bring about a situation in which the three Western powers might tire of the abnormal difficulties involved in protecting West Berlin against conversion into a Free City as well as Adenauer's intransigence. Soviet invitations to the West to conclude the last war by a peace treaty, to trade, to exchange visits, to coexist, and to disarm may all be regarded as instrumental in bringing about such a situation.

But in this general effort toward a *détente*, the Soviet denial of Adenauer's right to concern himself with West Berlin was the most interesting, and potentially the most dangerous, aspect of the new Soviet tactic. It was dangerous to the economic well-being of the city, which depends on its ties with West Germany, and to the Western presence in Berlin and thus to Berlin's political freedom. It also endangered, by implication, the cohesion of NATO, since West Germany would be a less reliable ally if it felt that the major NATO powers had not adequately protected their interest in West Berlin.

In its new tactic, the Soviet Government concentrated with remarkable ingenuity on a link in the alliance between the Federal Republic and the Western powers that is weak, because the legal grounds of the relationship between West Berlin, West Germany, and the three major Western powers are variously interpreted among them.

To repeat, the new tactic permitted the Soviet Government to concede explicitly that the Western powers had occupation rights in Berlin for the time being. The West's insistence on these rights and its objections to an ultimatum had been the two stands in the crisis that the Western powers had taken with great ardor and strong moral conviction. On both of these points, the Soviet Government appeared to be more conciliatory. But it did not need to press them in order to pursue its old interests in the removal of the Western powers from Berlin (and, if possible, from West Germany), in Western recognition of the German Democratic Republic, and in the disintegration of NATO. The Soviet leaders probably believed that the successful defamation of the Bonn Government would facilitate an interim settlement of the Berlin issue and undermine the Western alliance system. It was known to the Russians that the Adenauer Government opposed an interim settlement, which was often referred to in the West German and West Berlin presses as the *status quo minus*. It was also known to the Russians that the British Government had not dismissed the possibility of finding an interim solution, possibly along the lines of the last Western Geneva proposals. Anything the Soviet Government could do to reduce Adenauer's influence and credit in Western councils was therefore in the Soviet interest. This is still true today.

The new Soviet tactic at the very least increased concern among the Berliners as to what the future might hold for them, and at best (from the Soviet vantage point) shook the confidence of West German businessmen in Berlin's future. But without the determination of the Berliners to stay free, and without the economic and political support of the Federal Republic, Western troops could not, in the long run, protect the city from slow strangulation.

The danger of the new Soviet tactic was noticed by German observers, particularly in Berlin:

A clear new line can be discerned in Soviet foreign policy: Linked with friendly words and gestures inviting relaxation directed at the West are sharp attacks on the Federal Republic. . . .[18]

After having failed to "demilitarize" West Berlin, the Kremlin now tries to isolate the free part of our city politically and economically.[19]

Khrushchev has learned something in the last few months. . . . His attack is no longer directed against the rights and the presence of Allied troops but against the rights and the presence of the Federal Republic in the German capital.[20]

In particular, Mayor Brandt and some of his closest advisers, such as the Berlin Senator for Federal Affairs, Guenter Klein, warned that the Soviet attack was designed to sever the vital cord between the Federal Republic and West Berlin.[21]

10

Berlin and Bonn

THE DIVERGENCE OF OPINIONS on the legal status of West Berlin, which the Soviet tactic tries to exploit, results from an inevitable conflict of interests between the Federal Republic and the Western powers, which are present in West Germany as NATO allies but in West Berlin as victors in World War II.

Berlin has been under military occupation by the four major powers since 1945. After the Berlin blockade of 1948–49, however, the city was divided and the four-power administration was suspended. This left West Berlin under tripartite Western administration. In 1949–50, when the Federal Republic was constituted, the status of West Berlin in relation to the new West German state was dealt with in Articles 23 and 144 of the Basic Law of the Federal Republic, which was drafted by a Parliamentary Council. These Articles treated West Berlin as a *Land* (state) of the Federation, but when the Allied Military Governors approved the Basic Law on May 12, 1949, they made certain reservations regarding the meaning of the two Articles. The reservations were to the effect that although the representatives of Berlin are permitted to attend the meetings of the legislative bodies of the Federal Republic (Bundestag and Bundesrat), they may not vote, and that Berlin may not be governed by the Federation.[1]

By these reservations, the Allied authorities wanted to forestall a Soviet denunciation of the Protocol of September 12, 1944, which provided for the joint occupation of Berlin, but not for any right to dispose of the occupation sectors of Berlin. In connection with such a denunciation, a Soviet attempt might well have been made to justify a termination of Western rights of access to Berlin. As early as February, 1949, when it became known that the Parliamentary Council had resolved to integrate West Berlin as the twelfth *Land* in the Federation, the Information Buro of the Soviet Military Administration in Germany declared:

> The provocative and adventurous character of this resolution consists in the conscious neglect of the fact that Berlin can only be the capital of a unified German state and that it can in no case be included in a

70

separate West German state, since it lies in the Soviet occupation zone and is connected with it.

The resolution . . . proves that certain aggressive German circles try to exploit "the Berlin Question" for increasing the frictions between the occupation powers in Germany and that they also try to convert Berlin into a hotbed of economic and political acts of diversion against the Soviet Zone of occupation. . . .[2]

On August 29, 1950, the Allied Kommandatura approved the Berlin Constitution and suspended paragraphs 2 and 3 of Article 1, which said that Berlin is a *Land* of the Federal Republic and that the Basic Law and the laws of the Federal Republic are binding on Berlin.[3] A Federal law can now be adopted in Berlin only if it contains a so-called cover law and is enacted by the Berlin Chamber of Deputies. Although such an enactment does not require Allied approval, it can be suspended or declared invalid by the Western Commandants.[4] Federal treaties are enacted in Berlin by a similar procedure.

The Allied Kommandatura remained the governing authority in Berlin and maintained certain rights, powers, and responsibilities in that city when the occupation of Western Germany came to an end on May 5, 1955. In particular, the Berlin police remained under the command of the Allied authorities. The Allied authorities also have the right to take such emergency measures "as are necessary to fulfill their international obligations, ensure public order, and maintain the status and security of Berlin. . . ." [5]

Thus, at the time when West Germany was permitted to join NATO, the occupation powers became the allies of the Federal Republic, but in Berlin their status did not change. They committed themselves, however, to "consult with the Federal Republic in regard to the exercise of their rights relating to Berlin." The Federal Republic, on its part, is obligated to "co-operate with the three Powers in order to facilitate the discharge of their responsibilities with regard to Berlin." [6]

Although the Allied Kommandatura has never changed its view that West Berlin is not a *Land,* West Berlin has been treated by the Allies in many respects as if it were a full member of the Federation. The Allied powers have welcomed West German aid to Berlin's deficit economy; they have tolerated the operation of Federal agencies in Berlin and have fostered the development of other close ties between the Federal Republic and the former capital of the Reich. Without these ties, West Berlin would not be what it is today, the show window of the West behind the Iron Curtain.

The direct Federal contributions that Berlin receives from the Federal Government amount to approximately 1 billion Deutsche Marks per year.[7] Berlin, like the other *Länder,* also benefits from various Federal services, which include annually about 200 million DM for occupation costs, 150 million DM in relief for war victims, 360 million DM for indemnities to victims of Nazi persecution, 260 million DM for social insurance, 150 million DM for public-employee pension grants, 100 million DM for housing construction, of which a large part is for refugees from the Soviet Zone, etc.[8] The West Berliners also enjoy certain tax preferences, preferential shipping rates, and other special advantages.

With the help of the Federal Government, West Berlin has participated in the economic prosperity of West Germany. From 1950 to 1958, its production rose from 3.9 billion DM to 8 billion DM. Taking production in 1936 as 100, the production index rose from 32 in 1950 to 118 in 1958.

Apart from an initial shock, the political crisis that began in November, 1958, has not affected the economic life of West Berlin unfavorably. In addition to the aid provided by the Federal Government, West Berlin's economy received direct support from West German industry. By November, 1959, the production index had reached 152.[9] Unemployment in West Berlin, although a little higher than in West Germany, today amounts to less than 4 per cent of the gainfully employed, which is less than half of what it was prior to November, 1958. Savings accounts, which were adversely affected in the first two months of the crisis, continue to rise; capital investments in the first half of 1959 were higher than in the previous year; and the rate of the number of

Germans emigrating from Berlin to West Germany has returned to normal. In short, Berlin has withstood the shock of the Soviet threat.

For many years, there has been a divergence of views between the Allies and Germans on Berlin's status. In Germany, the opinion prevails that Berlin is a *Land* in which the Federal Government cannot exercise those functions the Allied powers have prohibited. In Allied opinion, this interpretation reverses rule and exception: Allied authority is supreme, but the Federal Government exercises certain functions in Berlin with the explicit or tacit permission of the occupation authorities. As early as 1949, West German jurists advanced the theory that West Berlin is *de jure* a member of the West German Federation.[10] Others have gone even further and have claimed that in the course of time a *de facto* membership as well has developed.[11]

In normal circumstances, these differences in legal interpretation of Berlin's status would present no difficulties. But in the present international crisis, they may. The new Soviet attack on the relationship between Bonn and Berlin attempts to use the legal doctrine of the Western allies against the factual integration of West Berlin into the political, economic, and legal order of West Germany, an integration that has been fostered by the Allies as well as the Germans. When the Soviet Government adopted its new tactic, it was Willy Brandt and his spokesmen who urged most strongly that the Western powers should defend the freedom of West Berlin on the grounds that Berlin was a *Land* of the Federal Republic—though a *Land* of a special kind—and that since the ties between West Germany and Berlin had developed with Allied approval, they should not be severed. Brandt appeared to underestimate the risks of such a stance. If the Allies had taken it, they would have diminished the international value of their occupation rights, on which their presence in Berlin rests. If the Federal Government had adopted Brandt's views, this might have led to increased friction among the Western allies, from which only the Soviet Union could have profited. In the end, Brandt assumed a somewhat more guarded position. On January 7, 1960, he presented a Five Point Declaration in the Berlin Chamber of Deputies summarizing his views on the Berlin crisis. A few days later, when Adenauer visited Berlin, the Chancellor declared that he fully agreed with these principles: [12]

1. The presence of the Western powers in Berlin and their rights are based on the total capitulation of Germany. . . .

2. West Berlin belongs to the free part of Germany. The integration of Berlin in the legal, financial, and economic systems of the Federation, which has occurred in the past ten years with the knowledge and the approval of the Western powers, is a basic condition for the existence of our city in freedom. . . .

3. The free access from and to Berlin must not be restricted, but should be perfected and improved. . . .

Brandt pointed out that for the Western powers such free access was a part of their occupation rights, and that the four powers had agreed at the end of the Berlin blockade, in 1949, that the movement of persons and goods and the exchange of information between the Western zones and the East Zone and between Berlin and the zones were to be *improved*. In this regard, Brandt did consider the possibility of doing more than maintaining the *status quo*. He concluded point 3 by saying:

We would welcome it if the right of free access to Berlin would be strengthened by more specific agreements.
    4. Any possible agreement concerning Berlin must not fail to take account of the will of the Berlin population. . . .

This reference to the right of self-determination was in line with Adenauer's emphasis on this right in general.

Point 5 was a weakly phrased plea for maintaining Berlin as a place where Germans from East and West could meet freely.

Early in February, 1960, before the Communist People's Chamber, Otto Grotewohl again advanced a legal claim to West Berlin. In Moscow, he was supported by a prominent Soviet authority on international law, Professor G. Tunkin, who had been one of Gromyko's advisors at the Geneva Conference. Soon thereafter, at his press conference in Jakarta, Khrushchev himself declared flatly, "West Berlin is located on the territory of the German Democratic Republic." [13] On January 18, 1960, *Die Welt* had advanced the thesis that West Berlin was part of the Federal Republic,[14] deriving this claim from the West German Basic Law of May 8, 1949, from the Four Power Agreement of 1949 that dealt with Western access to Berlin, and from various other postwar agreements. Taking issue with this article, Professor Tunkin argued skillfully and correctly that the three Western powers had never stated that they regarded West Berlin as part of the Federal Republic. Instead, the Allied Kommandatura had taken precisely the opposite view, as had the French Foreign Minister, Couve de Murville, at the Geneva Conference. Finally, Tunkin claimed that in September, 1944, Berlin had not been declared a special zone of occupation but had been assigned a special status within the Soviet Zone of occupation. One of Tunkin's arguments was based on the fact that the section of the Protocol of September 12, 1944, that dealt with Berlin was headed "Administration of Greater Berlin," so that the special status of Berlin was only of an administrative nature. He overlooked the fact that the content of this section clearly indicated that Berlin was to be "occupied" and not merely "administered."

Tunkin's article caused a minor stir in Bonn, and *Diplomatische Korrespondenz,* which is close to the German Foreign Office, set out to refute Tunkin's arguments. On March 29, 1960, the Department of State republished the wartime Protocol of September 12, 1944, with comments. The Department declared that Allied forces had remained in Berlin "without relinquishing the rights derived from the military defeat of Nazi Germany" and that

> There is, therefore, no basis for suggesting that Berlin has somehow been mysteriously merged with or placed on the territory of one of the occupation powers.[15]

11

Status Quo?

IN DECEMBER, 1959, the chiefs of state of the three Allied powers and of the Federal Republic reaffirmed once more their resolution to maintain Western rights in Berlin. A communiqué on the deliberation at this so-called Western summit meeting, issued on December 21, endorsed the Four Power Declaration and the NATO Declaration of December, 1958. The new communiqué contained no reference to the possibility of an interim solution of the Berlin issue, which the West had suggested at Geneva in July.

The Bonn Government was reported to be jubilant. It was known, however, that the United Kingdom and some smaller NATO powers, such as Denmark and Norway, still favored an interim solution for Berlin

79

and believed that it could be negotiated at the summit meeting.

On January 11, for the first time addressing the Berlin Chamber of Deputies, Adenauer stated in very blunt terms not only that it would be false in his view to resume negotiations at the summit at the point where the Geneva negotiations were broken off, but also that the Western proposal of July 28, 1959, had been rejected and therefore "no longer existed." [1] If Soviet demands on Berlin were met, "new demands would follow today, tomorrow or the day after tomorrow. And the first capitulation will then be followed by other capitulations." Pleading for unity, Adenauer said that the Berlin crisis concerned not only the city itself, but also "the freedom of the whole German people and the freedom of Western Europe as well." [2]

Adenauer's speech was attacked not only by the Soviet Union but also in Great Britain, especially by the socialists. Tass spoke of "Adenauer's demonstrative arrival in West Berlin, which never belonged to the Federal Republic, does not belong to it now, and lies in the midst of the German Democratic Republic." It added that evidently "the Bonn government has no interest in the forthcoming summit meeting." [3] Following Khrushchev's lead in his speech of January 14, 1960, Soviet propaganda against West Germany increased in vehemence. "It can be said without any exaggeration," wrote the Soviet specialist of the *Neue Zürcher Zeitung,* "that Khrushchev's regime is determined to destroy democracy in Germany, just as the early Stalin regime did in the Weimar Republic." [4]

In some British quarters Adenauer was described after his speech as "a tiresome old man," [5] and in April the British socialist Denis Healy wrote:

> It is now almost universally believed in Britain that Chancellor Konrad Adenauer is the main obstacle to any agreement with Russia at the forthcoming summit meeting.[6]

In February, when Selwyn Lloyd admonished the socialist opposition in the House of Commons to cease its participation in the Soviet campaign of defamation against Adenauer, he was interested in blocking British support of the Soviet attempt to isolate the Federal Republic from its allies, but at the same time he appeared to share some of the premises underlying the socialist attack on Adenauer. He did not criticize the socialist opposition for attributing aggressive intentions to Germany, but suggested instead that it was politically desirable to tie Germany to the West in order to safeguard peace.[7]

In West Germany, too, there were some skeptical and critical press comments on Adenauer's attitude,[8] although on the whole, public reaction was favorable. From the beginning of the crisis, government and op-

position have been united on the Berlin issue most of
the time, however much they differ on many other
aspects of foreign or domestic policy. It must be added,
however, that at least at the beginning of the crisis, this
unity tended to exhaust itself in demands for Western
firmness. Like the Adenauer Government, the Socialists
wanted the Western powers to remain in Berlin.
Naturally, the fate of Berlin is of more immediate concern to the Germans than the future of Quemoy. At
the beginning of the Berlin crisis, some Social Democrats, who had condemned "atomic death" and American defense policies only a short while before, privately
admitted to putting their trust in the deterrent power
of the American nuclear forces. But on the relation of
the Berlin issue to the question of German unification,
disagreement between the Christian Democrats and the
Socialists was as strong as ever. The Social Democrats
tried for a while to associate the resolution of the Berlin
issue with military disengagement, and it is not impossible that such ideas will regain importance in the
future.[9]

The agreement of government and opposition parties
on Berlin has been buttressed by co-operation between
the Christian Democratic Chancellor and the Socialist
Mayor of Berlin. Ever since the Geneva Conference,
this co-operation has become quite close. At the time
of Adenauer's address in Berlin, in January, 1960, the
two leading German politicians gave an impressive dem-

onstration of unity. The Chancellor emphasized, more than did Brandt in his speech, the relationship between Berlin and the Western allies. The Mayor, on the other hand, put special stress on the relationship of the city with the Federal Republic and spoke of Berlin as an "integral part of free Germany." But this may have been an intended, complementary rather than divisive, difference in emphasis. It is fortunate that both the present Mayor of Berlin and the former Mayor of Cologne are aware of what is at stake in the Berlin crisis not only for the freedom of the Berliners and the stability of the West German regime, but for the security of the West as a whole.

At the beginning of the crisis, it sometimes appeared that Berlin, in true appreciation of the real balance of power, looked to Washington rather than Bonn in order to read the signs of the future. But Berlin is dependent on the Federal Republic not only economically but also politically. The Bonn Government represents Berlin in the Allied councils that define Western policy vis-à-vis the Soviet Union. Hence Brandt's interest, regardless of party differences, in a united front with Adenauer vis-à-vis the Western allies.

As for the Chancellor, he can use the Mayor in negotiations with his allies, particularly if he should want support in resisting any Western proposals to change the *status quo;* and in the event that Adenauer's resistance should prove to be futile, close association with Brandt would enable him to deflect Socialist criticism. Similarly, if his own policy on Berlin were not supported by Brandt, he could try to blame the Mayor for any developments that he, the Chancellor, was unable to prevent. As we shall see presently, such a situation arose when Adenauer proposed in Washington that a plebiscite be held in West Berlin and Brandt appeared to demur.

In February, 1960, the German press announced that the Bonn Government would make available to its allies a new memorandum on Berlin in which the legal aspects of the situation would be set forth once more. A Berlin paper remarked dryly that the Federal Government considered it necessary to take this action "because a certain lack of clarity had proved to exist during the Foreign Ministers' Conference at Geneva in the previous summer." [10] The memorandum dealt not only with the illegality of the Communist threat against the Western presence in Berlin but, taking account of Mayor Brandt's interests, also with developments that led to the present close dependence of Berlin on the Federal Republic. In addition, the memorandum stressed especially that the Allied powers must consult the Bonn Government before reaching any new agreement with the Soviet Union.

The question arises why such a memorandum was prepared at that juncture. Since the Western allies had consulted Adenauer on all aspects of the crisis, documenting the need for such consultation may appear as a gratuitous gesture. A neutral observer in Bonn reported that "Occasionally one senses even a trace of annoyance [on the part of the Allies] at the distrust which Bonn's current legal preoccupation seems to betray." [11] But for all his evident reliance on association with, and protection by, his Western allies, especially the United States, Adenauer has never lost sight of the fact that under certain unfavorable circumstances, a *détente* between the Western powers and the Soviet Union might occur. He has often warned the Bundestag to that effect. In the past, such warnings were dismissed by the opposition as tactical moves of the wily Chancellor to gain parliamentary support for his controversial defense policies. Since the end of the war, however, German political self-assurance has never been strong. Some Germans believe that the Chancellor has been uneasy since he learned, directly upon his return from Washington and only after the passage of the German Conscription Law in July, 1956, of the so-called Radford Plan to reduce the strength of American ground forces.

In any event, the Berlin crisis had produced a series of reminders that the policies of the Allies might change. Take the Western proposal, made at Geneva, that the Allies would accept East German authorities as agents of the Soviet Union controlling Western military traffic to Berlin. When Secretary Dulles first alluded to such a possibility at a press conference in

November, 1958, Foreign Minister von Brentano called Dulles' remarks "incomprehensible." Similar consternation was caused by an observation Dulles made in January, 1959, that "free elections" were not necessarily the only way to achieve German unification; by Macmillan's visit to Moscow; and by the warm reception Mikoyan was given by some American businessmen.[12] In the middle of January, 1959, the Chancellor had no less than three top-level representatives in Washington, all apparently trying to ascertain whether or not American policy on Berlin was changing. In Geneva, Western representatives were reported to have intimated in private conversations that for reasons of domestic policy in the Western countries, especially in the Federal Republic, diplomatic recognition of Ulbricht's regime was impossible for the time being.[13]

After the Geneva Conference, it was especially Khrushchev's visit to the United States that revived Bonn's anxieties. In the meantime, fear was allayed by new Western assurances and particularly by the communiqué issued at the Western summit meeting in December, 1959. There still remained considerable uncertainty, however, as to what was going to happen at the summit. Since Great Britain and, to a lesser extent, the United States indicated their interest in seeking a settlement that would improve the Western position in Berlin,[14] Adenauer and Brandt were concerned that a *status quo plus* was likely to be unacceptable to

Khrushchev and that the Allies might be persuaded to accept a solution that would establish a *status quo minus* from the German point of view. Hence Adenauer's fixation on maintaining the *status quo* and his preoccupation with international legal matters rather than with the military aspects of the situation. Hence, too, his and Brandt's reminder that the will of 2.2 million free Berliners must never be disregarded.

At the end of his visit to the United States in March, 1960, Adenauer suddenly proposed that a plebiscite be held in West Berlin prior to the summit meeting so that the population itself could express its views on the Communist plan to turn Berlin into a Free City. The Chancellor made this allegedly improvised proposal after he had seen President Eisenhower. The response to the proposal was mixed. Evidently the West Berliners almost to a man would cast their votes in favor of affiliation with the West, but this fact had long been known from the results of political elections. The last election, held on December 7, 1958, shortly after the Soviet ultimatum had been issued, had been a crushing defeat for the Communists, and this result had been widely hailed as an expression of the ardent wishes of the Berliners that the ultimatum be rejected. What then was the point of Adenauer's proposal? Holding a plebiscite could be construed as a fatal admission of the occupation powers that the right of their presence in Berlin was invalid. Did Adenauer want to impress the

Communists? If so, the most astute answer was given in Bonn by Soviet Ambassador Smirnov, who commented that despite the progress that had been made in Geneva toward a settlement of the Berlin issue, the Bonn Government demanded the right of self-determination for Berlin and wanted at the same time to see the occupation continue. "But the statute of occupation and the right of self-determination exclude one another like fire and water." [15]

Other observers remarked that in proposing a plebiscite in Berlin, the Chancellor was prompted by doubts of American firmness, or more specifically by dissatisfaction with the outcome of his talks with the President. A leading German newspaper reported that when the Chancellor saw the President, he was ready to occupy successively three lines of resistance to any possible change at the summit of the *status quo* in Berlin: (1) no negotiations whatever about Berlin; (2) negotiations, but no agreement; and (3) a new agreement in which neither the occupation rights of the Allies nor the will of the Berliners would be compromised. When Adenauer found himself at the third fall-back position, he went over to "the counteroffensive" by proposing the plebiscite.[16]

The Social Democrats and the Free Democratic Party criticized the Chancellor's venture for various reasons. To begin with, as an embittered opposition, they find fault with everything Adenauer does. In addition, they resented the fact that Mayor Brandt, who had previously mentioned the possibility of a plebiscite as a last resort, had not been consulted by the Chancellor in this case. Finally, they claimed to be apprehensive that the Chancellor's initiative could be interpreted as an expression of mistrust in Germany's allies.[17] The Berlin press commented on the proposal without attacking the Chancellor,[18] but the Berlin Senate did nothing to support Adenauer's initiative. A spokesman of the Berlin Senate observed that after the summit meeting, a situation could arise in which the Senate itself might want to initiate a plebiscite.[19] Mayor Brandt first declared in Munich that Berlin was ready for a plebiscite "if it were desired by the Big Powers," [20] and added later that in the event of a plebiscite, the population of the whole city and not only that of West Berlin would have to participate.[21] He was also known to believe that a sharp instrument like the plebiscite should not be prematurely blunted.[22] It soon became apparent that Adenauer was angry because his idea was not supported by Mayor Brandt and the Berlin Senate.

In the meantime, the Communists had kept the threat to Berlin alive, but not without simultaneously using more engaging means of persuasion. Soon after Khrushchev's aggressive speech to the Supreme Soviet in January, 1960, the Department of State let it be known that at a New Year's Eve party in the Kremlin the Soviet dictator had accused the West of stalling on the Berlin issue and other international questions.[23] If the Western powers believed that they could postpone a settlement of the Berlin issue from one summit meeting to the next, he would, in due course, go ahead and sign a separate peace treaty with East Germany. Thus pressure was increased again despite the spirit of Camp David.

In February, the Warsaw Pact countries met in Moscow and included in their communiqué the threat of a separate peace treaty, again without any specific date. Earlier warnings that the German Democratic Republic might be equipped with atomic weapons in retaliation to West German defense measures were not mentioned in the communiqué, and it is possible that for once the Pankow Government had overreached itself with its propaganda that Adenauer was preparing for a blitzkrieg toward the East.

Similarly, when President Gronchi visited Moscow, Khrushchev treated him rudely and again threatened to conclude a separate peace treaty.[24] On February 8, Secretary Herter was asked at his press conference if Khrushchev had become "tougher" in the last three months. He replied, "Yes, I think that is the only way we can interpret the statements that have been made since that time." [25] And the Secretary referred specifically to the declaration at the Warsaw Pact meeting. Later at the same conference, the Secretary stated in reply to another question that "the spirit of the agreement reached at Camp David" would "certainly [be] violated" if the threat of a separate peace treaty were implicitly or explictly made before there was a full opportunity to discuss Berlin at the summit. Finally, when asked whether "what Khrushchev or the Warsaw Pact people have said so far" constituted such a violation, he replied, "No, because they have not put any time limit on this at all." [26]

Thus, in order not to foreclose the possibility of an understanding, the seriousness of the Communist threat was again associated with the ultimatum rather than the threat itself.

While the Communists insisted again that they would sign a separate peace treaty with the German Democratic Republic if they failed to reach agreement with the West, they intimated, in particular through Ambassador Smirnov in Bonn, that they regarded the Western proposal for an interim settlement of the Berlin issue, made at the end of the Geneva Conference, as a basis for further negotiations at the summit. In January, 1960, Smirnov tried to break up the solidarity regarding Berlin between Adenauer and the Social Democratic Party and between that party and Mayor Brandt by approaching the Social Democratic leaders Erich Ollenhauer and Herbert Wehner with information designed to suggest possibilities for reaching a compromise on Berlin. The attempt was not entirely unsuccessful. On February 22, 1960, the Social Democratic Party urged the Federal Government to use diplomatic channels for an inquiry into the meaning of certain points made in the document that Smirnov had presented to Ollenhauer and Wehner. The Federal Government refused to do so, declaring that it regarded the document primarily as an effort to destroy the unity of the German political parties on Berlin.

But Smirnov left no stone unturned. He also approached the Free Democratic Party, and on March 22, 1960, at a press conference in Bonn, he declared again that although the Western proposal of July 28 for an interim settlement had been rejected by Gromyko, "negotiations about it have not been exhausted." [27]

Similarly, Khrushchev himself made at least one curiously restrained statement when he visited France. At his press conference at Rambouillet on April 2, 1960, he declared that it would be "very undesirable" for the Soviet Government to sign a separate peace treaty with the German Democratic Republic. "We should like not to do so," Khrushchev said. "But if there is no other way out we will be impelled" to take this step. And he added, of course, that this step would lead to the loss of all Western rights in Berlin.[28] Early in April, 1960, General de Gaulle was reported to have told the British that Khrushchev would not press the Berlin issue to the point of crisis at the summit meeting. Such reports were unconfirmed,[29] but their mere existence indicated that Khrushchev's effort to appear reasonable had not been entirely wasted.

While the Communists made these seductive efforts at diplomatic persuasion, they continued to test and weaken the Western powers in Berlin by various maneuvers, none of which, considered in isolation, seemed to constitute a violation of the lofty spirit of Camp David, but each of which was designed to try the vigilance of the West and to wear down its resistance.

For example, in February, 1960, it became known that the application of a Scandinavian airline for commercial flights through one of the air corridors to West Berlin was granted by the Soviet representative of the Allied Air Safety Center with the notation on the document that this decision was made after the consent of the authorities in Pankow had been obtained. Thereupon, the Western representatives turned the application down, and the flight was redirected to Airport Schönefeld near Berlin.

Another incident occurred early in 1960, when the passports issued by the Soviet commander to the members of the Western military missions in Potsdam were suddenly changed to read that their bearers were registered residents of the German Democratic Republic. These missions in Potsdam, like the Soviet military missions in Frankfurt, Bünde, and Baden-Baden, had

93

been established at the end of World War II by special agreement among the four supreme commanders in accordance with the then-prevailing plan for a common administration of the whole of Germany.

While the issue did not directly involve Western occupation rights in Berlin, acceptance of the new passports would have meant a *de facto* recognition of the prerogative of the Pankow regime to change a four-power agreement. The Western military commanders wrote to the Soviet commander in Potsdam that they would under no circumstances accept the new documents,[30] but they did not warn him that they could close down the three Soviet military missions in West Germany as well as their own missions in Potsdam. According to a report from Berlin, Western observers pointed out that it was not advisable to give the Soviet Government "a pretext" for aggravating the situation.[31] But the Communists had not been deterred by this possibility from raising the issue in the first place.

The potentially most serious incident involved the altitude of Western flights in the air corridors to Berlin. The Communists had long sought to impose a ceiling of 10,000 feet on flights of Western aircraft in the corridors to Berlin. When an effort to that effect was made a year earlier, prior to the opening of the Foreign Ministers' Conference in Geneva, the U.S. Government had protested sharply in a note delivered to the Soviet Foreign

Ministry on April 13, 1959, that "the United States nĕver has recognized and does not recognize any limitations to the right to fly any altitude in the corridors." Prior to the summit meeting in Paris, the Communists made another effort to force Allied aircraft to observe a low ceiling. Early in March, 1960, many newspapers reported that it had been decided in Washington to make a diplomatic protest reaffirming the Allied right to fly at any altitude. On March 8, however, President Eisenhower decided that the United States would not resume high-altitude flights for the time being, and no diplomatic action was taken. On the next day, Secretary Herter explained that a study of the problem had disclosed that there was "no operational necessity" for flights above the low ceiling. *The New York Times* commented that it was widely believed in Washington that the United States wanted to avoid "any unnecessary tension over the Berlin problem in advance of the coming East-West summit meeting." [32]

In the light of these incidents and discouraged by the failure of the three Western powers to take a firm stand specifically against the Soviet tactic of separating Berlin from the Federal Republic, many independent observers, particularly in Germany, grew increasingly pessimistic about the prospects of the summit meeting.[33]

But there were also signs that the West had remained alert. On April 3, it was reported that General Clyde D. Eddleman, Commander of the U.S. Army in Europe, was opposed to a reduction of the Western occupation forces in Berlin. He was said to have made vigorous and successful representations to Washington against any Western offer to reduce the strength of the Western 10,000-man force in West Berlin.[34] The American military authorities maintained that a reduction of Allied strength would endanger internal security in the city because of the possibility that Communist paramilitary units might infiltrate West Berlin as "civilian" demonstrators. This technique had been used by the Communists in 1947, and its potential danger was shown again in September, 1959, when the East Berlin Communists raised Communist flags over West Berlin subway stations and kept them flying for several days.

Prior to the summit meeting, two important official statements were made—by Secretary Herter in Chicago on April 4 and by Under Secretary Dillon in New York City on April 20. Herter rejected the Communist attack on Adenauer and chided Khrushchev for his refusal to apply the principle of self-determination to East Berlin and East Germany. In vague language, Herter mentioned the idea of "plebiscites" in Germany that could lead to an all-German government with which a peace treaty could be signed.[35] More important, however, was Herter's suggestion that progress toward new arms-control agreements was linked with Soviet policy on the German issue. If there should be Communist violations or threats of violation of the existing agreements on Berlin, "we can hardly move forward confidently in negotiating new arms control agreements with the Soviet Union." [36]

Dillon was even more forceful. The Berlin issue, he said, represented "a critical test of Soviet good faith." With his recent threats to sign a separate peace treaty, Khrushchev was "skating on very thin ice." Dillon termed the so-called German Democratic Republic "one of the outstanding myths in a vast communist web of prodigious mythology." If Khrushchev was really interested in liquidating the leftovers of World War II, was he prepared, Dillon asked, to remove Soviet forces from East Germany and the satellite countries? to grant self-determination to the East Germans and to the peoples of the Soviet-dominated states in Eastern Europe? to abandon "the fiction of a separate north Korea?" Dillon pointed out that the aim of the Paris meeting was "to minimize the risk of war of miscalculation." [37]

No doubt, Dillon's stanchness was an effort to improve the Western position in the forthcoming negotiations in Paris rather than an indication of unwillingness to negotiate. But Khrushchev did not choose to respond to Dillon's important statement that the Western powers were "willing to discuss interim arrangements to reduce tensions in Berlin." Instead, he attacked both Herter and Dillon. He refused to consider reunification as an appropriate topic for discussion in Paris, rejected again the suggestion of a plebiscite, and stated that Dillon was obviously violating the spirit of Camp David. Khrushchev reiterated his main threat that the Western powers "will forfeit the right of access to Berlin by land, water and air," if they refused to sign a peace treaty with the German Democratic Republic. The use of force to ensure the Western rights "will be countered by force." [38]

12

The U-2 Incident
and the Paris Conference

ON MAY 11, 1960, President Eisenhower joined the
circle of those Western statesmen who, in Khrushchev's
language, were violating the spirit of Camp David.
He officially sanctioned espionage activities conducted
against the Soviet Union as "a distasteful but vital
necessity." [1]

It is a time-honored practice of all countries to try to
collect intelligence secretly from other countries, but
it is also customary that the employment of spies be
officially denied in the event an agent is caught, because
sanction amounts to an official admission of a violation
of sovereignty. When the American U-2 aircraft came

down deep in Soviet territory, the U.S. Government seemed to observe this custom by issuing, on May 3, what the President later frankly called "a covering statement," [2] asserting that the U-2 airplane was a civilian aircraft engaged in weather reconnaissance. It became known, however, that the photographic instruments, the pictures taken with them, and the pilot had all been recovered by the Soviets. Thereupon, both Secretary Herter, on May 9, and the President himself, on May 11, justified the overflight as an action prompted by Soviet secrecy and by a sense of "responsibility" for protecting the American people and "free peoples everywhere" against the danger of surprise attack. Moreover, both of them stated that a program of such overflights had been in operation for four years.[3]

The U.S. note of May 12 to the Soviet Government did not deny the Soviet charges but acknowledged that "the collection of intelligence about the Soviet Union by American aircraft is a 'calculated policy' [an expression taken from the Soviet note of May 10] of the United States." It merely denied that the flights had any aggressive intent or that they were undertaken in an effort to prejudice the success of the summit meeting.[4]

Khrushchev claimed that he had been aware of these overflights for a long time. While this is not the same as saying that he had been aware of the quality and quantity of the intelligence obtained in this manner, the official American sanction of the espionage activity must have shocked him and given him cause to reflect on the balance of power. The official American sanction of the overflights, rather than the flights themselves, furnished strong proof of two vital facts bearing on the Berlin crisis. First, it demonstrated to Khrushchev more definitely than any other diplomatic statement could have done that the Communist policy of coexistence had not induced the U.S. Government to lower its guard. Khrushchev could not count on reaping the harvest of Camp David nor on his subsequent efforts to obtain concessions in Paris. Second, the official position taken by the U.S. Government immediately prior to the summit meeting must have appeared to Khrushchev as an act of America's confidence in its ability to defy with impunity Soviet power and saber-rattling.

Before he reached Paris, Eisenhower gave orders that the flights be discontinued. This was done, despite the previously stated defensive need for such flights, in the interest of avoiding responsibility for wrecking the summit conference, or perhaps in the interest of keeping the issue under political control and not allowing it to weaken the solidarity of the Allies.

Nevertheless, Khrushchev wrecked the summit meeting. In Paris, he demanded publicly not only assurances that U-2 flights would be discontinued, but also (1) their condemnation by the President as a method of espionage, (2) a public apology on behalf of the United States, and (3) punishment of all those who had any responsibility for this particular mission. Khrushchev combined these demands with a barrage of personal insults hurled at the President, which showed his bad manners rather than his power. He repeated this performance in a press conference in Paris after he had, in Eisenhower's words, "torpedoed the conference" because his extreme demands were not met. The President's trip to the Soviet Union was canceled.

There has been much speculation on the reasons for Khrushchev's action. The explanation that he was forced to do so by rivals for power in the Soviet Union can be safely dismissed.[5] President Eisenhower himself offered the explanation that even before the Soviet delegation left Moscow for Paris, it had been decided that "nothing constructive from their viewpoint would come out of the summit conference." [6] This is indeed plausible, although the point should not be stretched to mean that Khrushchev was looking for a pretext not to hold the meeting and found that pretext in the U-2 incident. For many years, he had ardently desired to meet the Western heads of state at the summit. While he could have obtained neither recognition of the East German Government in Paris nor a permanent change of the status of Berlin, until May 1 he might well have entertained hopes of gaining some concessions, however small, on the Berlin issue.

More interesting than his outburst in Paris was Khrushchev's behavior immediately afterward. It was known that on his return to Moscow, Khrushchev would stop in East Berlin. Many observers wondered how much further he would go in his apparent anger and frustration. Would he announce that the time had come for signing the treaty with the German Democratic Republic? If the German Communists were hoping for such a dramatic development, they must have been bitterly disappointed. "We are realists," said Khrushchev in his speech at the Werner-Seelenbinder Hall in East Berlin on May 20, 1960, "and we shall never follow an adventurous policy." [7] Khrushchev said that the question of the German peace treaty would be negotiated with the Western powers "in six or eight months." Thus, he declared a moratorium on the status of Berlin.

Careful reading of Khrushchev's speech gives the impression that the Soviet dictator covered up a tactical retreat. He recognized that the conclusion of the peace treaty agitated his Communist audience more than any other subject. He reaffirmed previous Soviet claims and then lashed out in a bitter and vulgar attack against Adenauer and Brandt.[8] Finally returning to the Berlin issue, Khrushchev exclaimed:

Of course, the Soviet Union and the other peace loving countries morally have every right to settle this matter without further delay by signing a peace treaty with the German Democratic Republic.[9]

103

Yet he derived even this "moral" right not from the U-2 incident, but merely from a fact that he was to stress more forcefully in Vienna a year later, namely, that the United States had concluded a separate peace treaty with Japan. How then did he make clear to his listeners why he would not exercise this right immediately? He said, "We have considered this question. And here is the conclusion we've come to." But again he hesitated. Instead of stating the conclusion at this point in his speech, he reiterated his belief that the peace-loving forces would prevail over the forces of reaction. Then he declared:

> *We would like to believe* that a summit conference will be held in six or eight months. Under these circumstances, it makes sense to wait still a little longer and try through the joint efforts of all four victorious powers to find a solution to the long-since-ripe question of the signing of a peace treaty with the two German states . . . [italics added].[10]

The expectations of his Communist listeners were allayed by the vague statement, "It won't get away from us. We'll wait. It will ripen better." From this trite consolation he finally drew the following conclusion:

> With respect to the German peace treaty, therefore, including the question of West Berlin, *it will evidently*

be necessary to preserve the existing situation until the heads-of-government meeting that, it is supposed, will take place in six to eight months [italics added].[11]

Evidently, Khrushchev was extremely cautious, if not timid. If he had decided to wreck the Paris conference because Herter's and Eisenhower's open endorsement of espionage activities had made it impossible for him to negotiate without loss of face with the Western statesmen, the decision he announced in East Berlin showed nonetheless that he did not dare to defy the United States by action rather than verbal insults. He not only abstained from executing the threat of signing a separate treaty, which he had uttered so often, but also said that such execution would be "adventurous"—in Communist parlance, a strongly pejorative term. Thus Khrushchev came very close to suggesting that the threat, while not necessarily adventurous itself, had been merely a tactical device for reaching a four-power agreement. Perhaps he had never been entirely content with the prospect of leaving so explosive an issue as the access rights to Berlin to his East German colleagues, who, after a separate treaty was signed, might negotiate with the Western powers about these rights without due regard for the dangers of the situation. Incidents might occur in such negotiations that could involve the Soviet Union in war with the West.

Such incidents were even more likely to occur if the Western powers refused to negotiate with "sovereign" East Germany and maintained their presence in Berlin. Indeed, in Khrushchev's estimate of the situation, the probability that events might take such a course must have been heightened by the U-2 incident.

The account of Khrushchev's behavior in Paris and East Berlin would be incomplete if no mention were made of one particular event that occurred on the night of May 15–16. Thomas S. Gates, U.S. Secretary of Defense, had given orders to the Joint Chiefs of Staff to test high-speed military communications in order to check the ability of the President, while abroad, to keep in touch with the Strategic Air Command and other military air forces in the United States. Simultaneously, both the Continental Air Defense Command and the Strategic Air Command gave orders for limited alerts, which were described, as is customary in such cases, as routine measures. The alert status lasted for seven hours.[12]

Considering the serious conflict over the U-2 incident, which had cast its shadow on the heads of state convening in Paris, the alert measures assumed special significance. The grave view that the U.S. Government took of the situation could still be gleaned after the conference from the report that Eisenhower gave to the nation. He, too, presented the test of communications as a routine measure. He did not mention the alert of the air commands, but he referred twice to Pearl Harbor and said that international negotiations had sometimes been used for concealing preparations for a surprise attack.

At his press conference in Paris on May 18, Khrushchev was asked by a reporter from the Communist broadcasting station in Berlin what he thought of this state of military alert. Khrushchev replied that he had not heard about it and then offered some fascinating comments, which throw much light on his views of the Cold War in general, and on both the U-2 incident and the Berlin crisis in particular.[13]

He said that if the situation was in reality as the reporter described it, then the alert was either a "provocation" or an act of "cowardice." If it was a provocation, it might have been undertaken "for the purpose of complicating the situation and, I would say, throwing a scare into the American people." In his next sentence, Khrushchev was no longer speculating, but simply assumed that he had detected the true motive of the measure:

> The hoodwinking of the Americans has been brought into play to make it easier to extract taxes from the people for military purposes.

This explanation suggests that Khrushchev was concerned with the possibility that by intensifying the conflict between the United States and the Soviet Union, he might have precipitated an arms race. "Provocation" in this context meant creating a favorable climate in the United States for increasing the American defense budget, and this was evidently a measure over which Khrushchev had no direct control. It also meant an attempt to provoke war either by inducing the Soviet Union to strike or by inducing the peace-loving forces in the West to throw caution to the wind and permit themselves to be controlled by militarist *provocateurs* who wanted war. In any event, *provocateurs* had "complicated" the situation by injecting into the conflict fear, anger, or other emotions that weaken human reasoning power in order to thwart the sober calculations required in the conduct of the Cold War.

Provocation by an enemy is feared by the Communists because it heightens the risk of their losing control over the future course of events.[14] Neither the American decision to go to war nor the American decision to increase defense expenditures was under Khrushchev's control, but only a third decision—his own—to embark or not to embark upon war.

Khrushchev's association of the alert with "cowardice" —the second explanation he offered of American motives—is therefore less startling than may first appear. In addition to the conscious arousal of anger and fear by *provocateurs*, inability to withstand the tension of political conflict may entail a loss of control over future events and thus lead to disaster. As Khrushchev put it, "*Provocateurs* provoke war, while cowards can sometimes start a war out of cowardice."

Khrushchev let his listeners infer that Secretary Gates, if not a *provocateur,* was simply a coward. "I do not know Gates or what he is worth." He continued by extolling the bravery of Marshal Malinovsky, who was sitting next to him at the time. Here was a hero, a leader in two wars, a man honored by many awards, and now the Soviet Minister of Defense. He said, "For him I can vouch. He is a staunch son of the Communist Party, a staunch son of his country."

At this point in the press conference, Malinovsky spoke up, "We have not declared any military alert."

And Khrushchev replied, "Correct. We have not declared an alert and will not declare one. Our nerves are strong."

Thus the Cold War is a war of nerves in which one may lose by succumbing to intimidation. Methods of intimidation "won't work on us," Khrushchev firmly declared, playing the role of another staunch son of the Communist Party. But Khrushchev may have realized, too, that one may also lose the war of nerves by intimidating the opponent too much, so that he will act frantically out of cowardly fear. Also, one may lose if enemy *provocateurs* succeed in accelerating the arms race to a pace one cannot maintain. Finally, one may lose if the *provocateurs* are given a pretext for starting a war recklessly. The last possibility has often been referred to in Soviet diplomatic notes and propaganda as the "madness" of imperialists.

This was Khrushchev's contribution in Paris to the theory of war by accident. When the risk of such war or of strengthening the opponent's defenses increases, it is imperative to be patient and to relax pressure on the opponent until he calms down and again becomes amenable to the conduct of the Cold War on Communist terms.

Whatever is the correct interpretation of Khrushchev's failure to sign a separate treaty after the U-2 incident and the abortive summit meeting, it appears that the fiasco in Paris was anything but a fiasco in regard to Western policy on the German and Berlin issues. It seems likely that Khrushchev had been jolted into heightened awareness of the risks involved in his policy.

In accordance with his statement in East Berlin, Khrushchev did not press for a summit meeting for several months. He seemed resolved to wait for the new American President to take office. He spoke on this subject again in an international press conference in New York on October 7, 1960, at the time of the meeting of the United Nations General Assembly. Referring to two discussions he had had with Prime Minister Macmillan, Khrushchev said: [15]

> We are in favor of a summit conference in order to resolve the question of concluding a peace treaty with Germany and turning West Berlin into a Free City.

He had expressed the idea to Macmillan, Khrushchev continued, "that it might be better to convene a conference of all of the competent countries" for this purpose. But since Macmillan had "assured" him that a summit conference would take place, Khrushchev concluded:

> In that case we abide by the promise we made after the United States thwarted the summit conference in May.

In reply to another question, Khrushchev also gave assurances that the *status quo* in Berlin would not be changed on the assumption that a summit meeting "must be held shortly after the election in the United States."

> But if we see that there is no desire to reach agreement [on holding a summit meeting], then those countries that understand the necessity of signing a peace treaty will assemble, a peace treaty will be signed, and that

111

will mean the end of the occupation regime in West Berlin, also.

In short, the resumption of Soviet diplomatic pressure for the conclusion of a peace treaty was postponed until some time early in 1961, although throughout 1960 Khrushchev kept alive his threat to conclude a separate treaty as an alternative to four-power agreement.[16]

13

Cold War by Proxy

DURING THE DIPLOMATIC MORATORIUM on the German and Berlin issues, Khrushchev continued his political attacks on the West and particularly on the United States. His threats against NATO bases increased in sharpness. He challenged the United States in its own hemisphere through rocket threats aimed at influencing U.S. policy toward Cuba. He tried American patience by his behavior in connection with the shooting down of the RB-47 airplane. While he was less successful in his attempts to exploit to his advantage the political chaos in the Congo, partly because the United Nations thwarted his designs, he made an intensive effort to rally the growing number of new states in Africa and Asia to form a third neutral bloc in the United Nations.

In this way, he hoped to paralyze this organization, and he even threatened to split it in the event the Western powers would not otherwise bow to his will. These political initiatives had no immediate bearing on the resolution of the Berlin issue, but Communist foreign policy is a global affair and its successes in Asia or South America contribute to what the Communists like to regard as the secular trend of their world-wide advance. Such successes also improve the chances of the Communists when they decide to resume their attacks in other parts of the world. In June, 1961, Khrushchev did not fail to convey to President Kennedy in Vienna his view that the global Communist position had been strengthened and his confidence that it would improve further in the future.

Nor were the Communists idle in Berlin during the period of the diplomatic standoff. They persevered in their efforts to isolate Bonn from Berlin and to create discord within NATO, particularly by attacking the Federal Republic. In these two respects as well, the Communists made further gains in the period between the high-level meetings in Paris and Vienna.

With regard to the Berlin issue, the moratorium may be characterized as a period of Cold War by proxy. While the Soviet Government concentrated on political trouble spots elsewhere in the world—the Congo, Cuba, the United Nations, and Laos—the pressure on Berlin was exerted primarily by the Ulbricht regime. By authorizing the German Communists to apply such pressure in carefully measured doses, Khrushchev consoled them about the fact that his own offensive had been temporarily halted. At the same time, these limited actions by proxy permitted him to probe further the resistance of the three Western powers and to wear it down if possible.

The Ulbricht regime regards East Berlin, and potentially the whole city, as the capital of the German Democratic Republic. In the Federal Republic, the whole of Berlin is considered to be the city that will become the capital when Germany is reunified, as it was Germany's capital before the country was partitioned.[1] In the meantime, however, the Communists have located the central agencies of the German Democratic Republic in East Berlin, while the Federal Government has taken certain actions to remind the West Germans and people abroad that West Berlin is the visible capital of the invisible Germany.

For example, in 1954 and 1959, the election of the President of the Federal Republic by the Parliament took place in West Berlin. Similarly, every year since 1955, the Bundestag had opened its session with a week's meeting in Berlin. It should be remembered that the Communist deputies in the West German Assembly (prior to the prohibition of the Communist Party in the Federal Republic) were the first to move that the Bundestag hold meetings in Berlin, doing so as early

115

as 1949. When the Bundestag met in Berlin for the first time, in 1955, *Neues Deutschland,* the official Communist newspaper, criticized the Bundestag for having taken so long to find its way to Berlin. Ever since the beginning of the Berlin crisis, however, both the Soviet Union and its German puppet regime have tried to deprive the city of its symbolic value as the future capital of free reunified Germany.

The annual Bundestag meetings in West Berlin have been characterized by the Communists as "provocations" and "Cold War measures." After the Paris conference Khrushchev personally addressed himself to this issue during his visit to Austria in July, 1960. At a press conference in Vienna, he threatened that if the Bundestag went ahead with its plans to hold a meeting in Berlin in September, he would "perhaps" sign a separate peace treaty, in which case, all West German deputies would have to ask Grotewohl for a visa in order to be able to return from Berlin to Bonn.[2]

The issue precipitated a controversy in West Germany and even strained relations between the political parties. Willy Brandt, the Social Democrats, and the Free Democrats were strongly in favor of holding the meeting, while Adenauer and the Christian Democratic Union maintained that caution was advisable. Ernst Lemmer, Minister of All-German Affairs, wrote that West Germany should not do anything that would make "unnecessary difficulties" for the Western powers that safeguarded Berlin.[3]

In the United States, Secretary Herter declared that the Bundestag should decide whether or not to meet in Berlin.[4] A similar position on this issue was taken by the British and French governments.

The meeting was postponed. In fact, not only the Federal Republic but also the three Western powers yielded to the Communists on an issue that the West did not consider of vital importance. It disregarded the fact that to the Communists *all* moot issues are of vital importance. They believe that every concession, however small, increases the chance of further concessions. When President Eisenhower declared at his news conference on August 10, 1960, that he did not think that a major Soviet move was contemplated against Berlin, he was entirely right, but he inadvertently obscured the danger of "minor" moves.

The German Communists made their next move against the celebration of a "Homeland Day" by West German organizations of expellees from the eastern regions of the former German Reich. The celebration was scheduled to take place in West Berlin from September 1 to 4. Both the Soviet Government and its German proxy had always tried to present the members of these organizations as unreconstructed nationalists and Irredentists who threatened Europe with war in order to reconquer the German territories lost in World War II. Ulbricht claimed that "the directives for the revanchist meeting came from the Bonn Government." [5]

On August 29, 1960, the government of the Soviet Zone prohibited visits of West Germans to East Berlin for the five-day period from August 31 to September 4. *The New York Times* referred to this incident as "the baby-blockade." The reason given for this measure was the preparations for celebrating Homeland Day in West Berlin. The Western allies were accused of permitting the military air corridors to Berlin to be misused for the chauvinistic purposes of German militarists, who were allegedly aided and abetted by the Federal Government. The German Democratic Republic declared that the meetings of the expellee organizations were "a new edition of the pernicious and disastrous demonstrations in which Goebbels used to announce total war."

> The only difference consists in the fact that this time it is not a matter of the conduct but of the preparation of total war. This situation obliges the government of the G.D.R. [German Democratic Republic] to state again that West Berlin does not belong to the Federal Republic and must not be governed by it. Neither the Bonn government and its agencies nor the organizations directed and financed by it have a right to be active in West Berlin. . . . The government of the G.D.R. calls the attention of the governments of the United States, Great Britain and France to the fact

that they carry full responsibility for all possible consequences of the misuse of the air corridors for the
transport of people who attend politically inciting
meetings in West Berlin.[6]

It should be noted that this time Ulbricht recognized
the Western right of access to Berlin, at least by implication, although this was merely a tactical device for
diverting the Western response to his move against German "militarism," and thus to discredit the Federal
Republic in the eyes of its allies. His hopes were not
disappointed. Many Western newspapers sharply criticized the Federal Government. There was talk about
"the exploitation" by the Federal Government of its
Western allies "for dubious aims." In these circumstances, the opinion could spread that Berlin might not
be worth defending.[7] At the very least, convening for
Homeland Day in West Berlin was not considered "prudent." [8] The political leaders of West Germany, it was
said, had done little to "relax the atmosphere at the
Iron Curtain." Moreover, they had occasionally created
confusion "among their own friends" abroad.[9]

It is quite true that in their effort to compete for the
votes of the expellees, West German political leaders
sometimes forget that patriotic Sunday speeches have a
shrill ring in the ears of many West Europeans and
Americans. The memory of Hitler, of World War II,
and of the atrocities officially sanctioned by a German

119

government in the not-too-distant past cannot be forgotten. German politicians must exercise a great deal of political tact and prudence, lest their actions erect an obstacle even greater than the fear of war to discourage the people of the West in the formidable political effort of defending Berlin; and political tact and prudence are rare virtues. The lack of such tact and prudence, however inadvertent or exceptional it may be, can never be explained quite satisfactorily as a misunderstanding on the part of those who take offense.

On August 28, 1960, a few days before Homeland Day, Vice-Chancellor Ludwig Erhard spoke to an audience of Silesian refugees in Düsseldorf, admonishing them not to forget their homeland, "German Upper Silesia," which, he said, still bore testimony to German rather than Polish life. This speech, like other similar Sunday speeches by German ministers and politicians of various political persuasions, instantly aroused sharp resentment in several Western countries.[10] Ulbricht's protest two days later against the celebration of Homeland Day in Berlin was, therefore, well timed.

After the rally had taken place, the whole British press, which generally is more critical of West Germany than the press of any other country, acknowledged that the celebration had been peaceful and calm.

On September 8, 1960, the Communists took another measure against West Berlin. The German Democratic Republic prohibited all citizens of the Federal Republic from visiting East Berlin in the future without a special permit; [11] and on September 13, the Council of Ministers in the Soviet Zone took a third measure, ruling that the passports of the West Berliners would no longer be considered as valid identification papers.[12]

The Western powers responded firmly. On September 12, 1960, they sent diplomatic notes to the Soviet Government protesting the new pressure from the Soviet Zone against Berlin. Certain retaliatory measures were taken against travel of the functionaries of the German Democratic Republic. In its replies of September 27, 1960, the Soviet Government again claimed that the Soviet Zone enjoyed the prerogative of laying down the rules on the movements of Germans in Berlin and between Berlin and the former zones of occupation. The Soviet Government also insisted that the three Western powers take the necessary measures "to prevent the revanchist activity in West Berlin" in the future and not to permit "the illegal use" of their access routes to Berlin. Finally, the notes again asserted that the four-power agreements made in the period of occupation had become invalid.[13]

Perhaps one of the most interesting aspects of the events in September was Ulbricht's attempt to isolate Bonn from Berlin not only by intervention in the affairs of West Berlin, but also by bypassing Bonn and approaching the West Berlin authorities directly. In his televised interview of September 3, 1960, Ulbricht declared that "the government of the GDR is always prepared for negotiations with the West Berlin Senate on the normalization of the situation in West Berlin." [14] The Communists left no stone unturned in order to disarray Western ranks. With this effort, Ulbricht merely followed in Khrushchev's footsteps. At the time of the latter's visit to Vienna in July, 1960, Gromyko had approached the Austrian Minister of Foreign Affairs, Bruno Kreisky, in the same manner. Gromyko was reported to have requested Kreisky to inform Willy Brandt of Khrushchev's desire to establish direct contact with the Mayor, because Brandt "was only insufficiently informed by Bonn and the Western powers." [15]

By September, 1960, it was clear that the tactical aim of the Communists was to erode the Western position in Berlin rather than to change the situation by a single political blow. In West Germany, this procedure was referred to as the "salami tactic," where the whole sausage eventually disappears, but in slow stages, slice by slice. It was also evident that for the time being, the Communist assault was conducted by the German Democratic Republic against the Federal Republic rather than by the Soviet Union against the three Western powers.

In these circumstances, particularly after the Soviet note of September 27, the Federal Government decided to take a more active role in the political struggle against the Soviet Zone. In the past, the Federal Government had looked askance at the possibility of applying economic sanctions against the Soviet Zone, partly because such pressure was judged to be effective only in the short run, and partly because it was feared that the Soviet Zone might take countermeasures against West Berlin, perhaps in the form of a new blockade. At the end of September, 1960, however, the Federal Government served "precautionary notice" to the German Democratic Republic that the interzonal trade agreement would expire at the end of the year. This step was taken to exert pressure on Ulbricht so that he would stop his illegal intervention in Berlin, particularly his restriction of the freedom of movement across the sectors of the city. The reaction of the Soviet Zone Government was surprisingly restrained, and in October, Ulbricht's pressure on Berlin relaxed.

The exact reasons for Ulbricht's sudden show of reasonableness are uncertain. It is possible that he acted upon Khrushchev's instructions. The Soviet leader again voiced his expectation that a new summit conference would be held in the spring of 1961 when he attended the United Nations General Assembly meeting in New York. Until then, he declared, no unilateral steps against Berlin would be taken. It is also possible that Ulbricht hoped to use the negotiations in December for a renewal of the interzonal trade agreement to make progress toward the *de facto* recognition by the Federal Republic of the "rights" he had usurped in Berlin.

Finally, it is possible that Ulbricht feared the consequences to the Soviet Zone's economy of a loss of West German imports.

In 1959, 11 per cent of the foreign trade of the Soviet Zone was with West Germany, an additional 14 per cent being accounted for by other Western countries. These relatively low figures obscure the fact that the imports of special steels and chemicals from West Germany are of great importance to the functioning of the Soviet Zone's economy. A discontinuation of these imports could cause serious disruption, and quick adjustments are impossible. Nor would it be easy for the Soviet Zone to find a market elsewhere for many of the products it exports to West Germany. In short, there is some evidence to suggest that the West German embargo on interzonal trade is a weapon in the struggle for Berlin of more than negligible importance.

14

Vienna: The New Offensive

THOSE WHO BELIEVE that summit diplomacy is useful to the Western powers in settling outstanding issues of the Cold War often point to the fact that Khrushchev's personal approbation is indispensable to any settlement with the Soviet Government. If lesser Soviet functionaries are recalcitrant in negotiations, it is hoped that their master will listen to reason and overrule them after he has talked with the Western heads of state. In order to find out whether a compromise can be reached with the Soviet Government, Khrushchev must be approached in person by men of his rank.

This view is faulty because there is no evidence to support the assumption that Khrushchev is more reasonable or more interested in compromise than, say,

Gromyko. It would be equally fallacious to assume
that Khrushchev orders Gromyko to be recalcitrant
merely to throw into relief his own true reasonableness
in later negotiations at the highest level.

Summit diplomacy is more advantageous to the Communists than it is to the Western powers. The most
important reason is not that the Communists are often
more successful in exploiting diplomatic events for
propaganda purposes than is the free world. The para-
mount Communist asset in summit diplomacy lies
rather in the overriding desire of the West to settle
international conflicts by compromise and live thereafter without fear of nuclear war. It is on the illusions
and frustrations that attend this desire that Communist
policy thrives. The Communists regard the settlement
of any issue as a ratification and a recognition of
the prevailing balance of military and political power.
Settlements merely brighten the prospect of further
gains in the continuing struggle with the West.

Moreover, summit diplomacy is a method of communication between sovereign states; it is not a policy.
When an international issue is troublesome, there is
need for a policy to make it less troublesome, but it is
by no means certain that an attempt to settle the issue
by compromise is the best policy; nor does the method
of negotiation ever meet the need for a policy.

Many experienced students of international relations
are skeptical of the gains to be reached by summit

diplomacy. For example, Secretary of State Dean Rusk has pointed out that "summit diplomacy is to be approached with the wariness with which a prudent physician prescribes a habit-forming drug." [1] He asked:

Have we not already made a major concession in yielding to a procedure which works to his [Khrushchev's] advantage and our disadvantage? [2]

Similarly, Wilhelm Grewe, the German Ambassador in Washington, observed, "For the Soviets . . . the mere occurrence of a summit conference is already a success." [3]

Throughout the history of the Berlin crisis, many British statesmen and politicians have favored summit diplomacy as a method of settling the issue. Apparently, they believe that summit meetings are as useful to the Western powers as they are to the Soviet Government, and that the East-West conflict can be reduced by Western concessions to Soviet policy on Germany.

In October, 1960, Macmillan again raised Communist hopes for a new summit conference when he talked with Khrushchev in New York. The Prime Minister repeated his suggestion a few days later in a speech at Scarborough in which he mentioned that the status of Berlin would have to be "negotiated" at the summit. Macmillan's statements caused concern not only in Berlin and Paris but also in the United States. In particular, Senator Kennedy, then a Presidential candidate, indicated that he would prefer negotiations to be conducted first on a lower plane, that is, by diplomats. Macmillan could hardly have expected a different attitude from any American, and especially from a candidate for the Presidency, if only in view of the rude personal insults President Eisenhower had received in Paris from Khrushchev.

In January, 1961, President Kennedy indicated again that he shared Dean Rusk's preference for exploring the possibility of lessening tension "through more traditional channels," [4] prior to a summit meeting. Two days later, however, Adlai Stevenson expressed his own "guess" that the President would welcome an opportunity to become acquainted with Khrushchev. Stevenson added that he himself would be "delighted" to see Khrushchev again, "because I have had many visits with him." [5]

Evidently, Stevenson was more interested in a get-acquainted meeting between Kennedy and Khrushchev than either the Secretary of State or the President himself. The same day on which Stevenson made his remarks, Pierre Salinger, the White House Press Secretary, commented that Stevenson "is expressing his own views," and Dean Rusk declared, also on the same day, "we intend to use our ambassadors fully." [6]

At that time, Llewellyn Thompson, the American Ambassador in Moscow, was engaged in negotiations with the Soviet Government. In the first months of the Kennedy Administration, hopes were running high that friendlier relations could be established between the United States and the Soviet Union than had prevailed in the last months of 1960, when Eisenhower was still President. Soviet propaganda dealing with the United States and President Kennedy was indeed more restrained than it had been in 1960.

On February 22, 1961, Ambassador Thompson tried to present a letter from Kennedy to Khrushchev, but he had to go to Siberia to deliver it. Kennedy awaited an answer to his letter for several months. Khrushchev's reply was presented by Ambassador M. Menshikov in Washington on May 16—after American policy had suffered serious setbacks in Laos and Cuba and after Kennedy had agreed to meet Khrushchev in Vienna. The meeting between the two heads of state took place without the diplomatic preparations on which Kennedy and Rusk had previously insisted.

However, it was stressed prior to and after the meeting, that the discussions in Vienna did not constitute a summit conference, but served only to enable two statesmen to get to know each other and their respective policy positions. It was also said officially in advance of the meeting that while the Berlin issue would come up at the talks in Vienna, it would not dominate them. Nevertheless, Kennedy's mere agreement to meet the Soviet leader was a tactical success for

Khrushchev, especially since Kennedy arrived in Vienna after the setbacks in Laos and Cuba and with no success in his foreign policy to back his stand.

In accordance with an *aide-mémoire* on the German peace treaty, dated June 4, 1961, Khrushchev impressed upon the President his determination to settle the German and Berlin issues before the end of the year. Thus he used the conference to seize the initiative, revive the Berlin crisis, and insist once again upon the urgency of its settlement according to his unchanged plans.

The West had been well advised, a few days before Ambassador Thompson tried to present Kennedy's letter of February 22 to Khrushchev and three and a half months prior to the Vienna meeting, that a new storm was coming. The signal consisted of the Soviet *aide-mémoire* of February 17, 1961, given by Ambassador Smirnov to Chancellor Adenauer. It remained unanswered for a long time.[7] This note, which was widely broadcast by the Soviet Union on March 3, urged the conclusion of a peace treaty for two principal reasons, first, the increasing demands being raised in West Germany for a "revision of the existing boundaries in Europe," as West German armaments were growing stronger, and, second, the "absolutely abnormal" situation in West Berlin. The note renewed the threat of a separate treaty with the German Democratic Republic "should the Federal Government still oppose a peaceful settlement with Germany." It also insisted again that the separate treaty would settle the status of West Berlin as a Free City. Finally, it pointed out:

> As in the past, the Soviet position does not exclude the possibility of a temporary settlement of the West Berlin question until a peace treaty with Germany has been concluded, provided that a specific time is set for the conclusion of such a treaty. It should be kept in mind that only the countries directly interested could participate in working out a temporary agreement on West Berlin and, of course, the Federal German Republic is not one of these.[8]

The note gave ample advance warning to the Western governments of what President Kennedy could expect to hear from Khrushchev in person. It was especially evident that the Soviet Government attached particular importance to the recognition of the Oder-Neisse Line.

Some of the most interesting passages of the *aide-mémoire* dealt with alleged Western attempts to delay negotiations on the peace treaty. These passages were written in a tone of sarcastic amusement:

> Evidently the West is now starting to realize the necessity for concluding a peace treaty, liquidating the state of war and normalizing relations between states. Nevertheless, some state figures are trying once again to set forth in negotiations such ideas as these: "Wait a moment; this is not the time. Preparations are under

131

way for the presidential election in the U.S.A. It is necessary to wait until it is over." After the election, they say: "The President and the new U.S. government have just taken up their duties and have not yet mastered them. Therefore it is necessary to let a certain amount of time pass." Others are reasoning that it is not yet time to decide this question because of the forthcoming elections in the F.G.R. [Federal Republic of Germany]. After elections in the F.GR., obviously, they also will say: "The elections have just taken place, and many irresponsible speeches were made in the dust of the election campaign. So again more time is required to let political passions subside and to let the inflammatory speeches be forgotten."

If matters are allowed to take this course, this can continue ad infinitum.[9]

In all essentials, Khrushchev repeated in Vienna the demands for a peace treaty with Germany and for turning West Berlin into a demilitarized Free City that had been familiar to the West since November, 1958. The *aide-mémoire* of June 4, 1961, did not contain an ultimatum but put the West under renewed time pressure. It declared that a peace conference should be called "without any delay," but if the Western powers were not ready to do so, the four powers should urge the two German governments to negotiate on questions within their authority pertaining to peace and reunification. For these negotiations, "a period not exceeding six months" [10] was stipulated. Thereafter, a peace treaty should be concluded either with both German states or with one of them, that is, with the Ulbricht regime.[11]

The televised report that Khrushchev made on June 15, 1961, on the Vienna meeting contained no reference to these phases of reaching a peace settlement. Instead, Khrushchev stated simply that "a peaceful settlement in Europe must be attained this year." [12] Strictly speaking, this statement was not an ultimatum either, but it put even greater pressure on the West than did the *aide-mémoire.*

In Vienna, Khrushchev also revived his proposal for a possible occupation of the Free City of West Berlin by forces of all four powers, which would mean that Soviet troops would enter West Berlin. And the *aide-mémoire* added that, alternatively, the Soviet Government would not object to troops of neutral countries being stationed in West Berlin under the auspices of the United Nations. The wording of this point was obscure. It was not clear whether the Soviet Government proposed that neutral forces be stationed in the city in addition to or in lieu of the token contingent of the four powers. Khrushchev clarified this point, however, in his speech of July 8, 1961, in which he specified three possible groups of military forces to be stationed in Berlin: (1) contingents of the four powers, (2) troops of neutral powers, and (3) U.N. forces.

The meaning of the renewed threat to Berlin was made cynically clear in a long news conference that

Ulbricht held immediately after the Vienna meetings. He stated that once Berlin became a Free City, he would close the West Berlin airport in Tempelhof and the centers in West Berlin that received the refugees from the Soviet Zone via East Berlin. The Western notes of July 17, 1961, addressed to the Soviet Government, pointed out that in view of Ulbricht's threatening statements, "it is not surprising if neither the West Berliners nor the Western powers are reassured by professions of peaceful intent." [13]

The significance of the renewed Soviet political offensive launched during the Vienna meetings lay not only in the solemnly repeated demands for a peace treaty and a new status for West Berlin, but also in the emphatic insistence on the immutability of the existing German borders. Following the spirit of the *aide-mémoire* that Smirnov had handed to the Federal Government on February 17, the new *aide-mémoire* stated bluntly that a peace treaty was necessary in order "to record the situation that took shape in Europe after the war, *de jure* to formulate the immutability of the existing German frontiers." [14] Khrushchev expressed this view even more strongly in his speech of June 15:

> There can be no question of any new changes of borders. We proceed from the premise that the peace treaty with Germany will put a seal on what has already been established by the Potsdam agreement. [15]

And again:

> Indeed the governments of the Western powers ob-
> viously understand, too, how senseless it would be to
> raise now the question of revising Germany's bound-
> aries. Their representatives have often told us of this
> during our conversations.[16]

Between June 4, the date of the Soviet *aide-mémoire,*
and July 17, 1961, the day on which the Western replies
were sent to Moscow, Khrushchev made no less than
three major speeches in which he poured new oil on the
fire he had relit. It became clear beyond any doubt that
the legal basis of the Western resistance to Soviet policy
did not impress him. Only the balance of military
power between the East and the West was significant.
The issue reduced itself in Khrushchev's mind to a
simple "recognition of the reality of the situation in
Europe." [17]

> Today, it is acknowledged in the West that the forces
> of the Soviet Union and the other socialist countries
> are not inferior to the forces of the Western countries.[18]

Khrushchev tried to convey the impression that the
Western powers would be simply unrealistic if they
failed to appreciate the true relationship between their
political ends and the means of reaching them that
were at their disposal. He suggested that the facts must

compel everyone "to heed the demand of the time and the voice of reason." [19] Only "facts," not rights or obligations, concerned him. Only facts were "normal."

Khrushchev did not seriously attack the leaders of the three Western powers in his statements. He reserved his venom for Chancellor Adenauer, who, he said, was "shouting himself hoarse for nuclear weapons," [20] and for Von Brentano, whom in one of the more frivolous flights of his imagination, Khrushchev compared with Von Ribbentrop, the architect of the nonaggression pact of 1939 between Hitler and Stalin. [21] However, Khrushchev did chide Macmillan, because he had called for "firmness," and De Gaulle, because of the French announcement that a division would be recalled from Algeria to Europe. But Khrushchev's criticism was restrained enough to indicate that he still hoped to exact concessions from the three Western powers in negotiations.

Khrushchev tried to placate the Western statesmen. The will of the Berliners would be respected. Their freedom would be guaranteed. There would be no blockade. He did not want to "affect the prestige of the United States, the United Kingdom, and France." [22] A four-power agreement on peace with Germany would make him "happier" than the conclusion of a separate treaty. [23] Recognition of the Ulbricht regime by the Western powers need not be linked with the conclusion of the peace treaty. [24] He spoke in a tone of sweet reason:

The Soviet Government agrees with President Kennedy's recent statement that any West Berlin solution must not infringe the rights of the population of this city to make an independent choice as free people.

Let us sit down at a table and calmly discuss all questions without resorting to threats.[25]

Khrushchev directed his attack primarily at the Western arguments, which he wanted to demolish, rather than at the Western statesmen, who, he hoped, would make concessions to him. He said that the Western policy of the reunification of Germany really meant "absorption," not reunification, and that Western professions of respect for self-determination made little sense in the light of Western policy in Vietnam. Nor had the Western powers any right to object to a unilateral peace treaty since they themselves had concluded such a treaty with Japan.[26]

No sooner did a Western suggestion for countering Soviet pressure gain attention in the Western press than Khrushchev tried to deflate it. He scorned American suggestions that diplomatic relations be broken off, that economic sanctions be applied, or that a partial mobilization of miltary manpower be ordered in the United States. All this was "nonsense" to Khrushchev rather than "commonsense." [27]

As always, Khrushchev tried to discourage the use of military force by the Western powers for maintaining their access to Berlin. The resort to force would be "banditry." [28] In the speech of July 8, in which he praised Viscount Montgomery for his public endorsement of military disengagement in Europe, Khrushchev also predicted that any Western resort to force would be rebuffed and that war unleashed by the imperialists would end "in the complete debacle and ruin" of the imperialist system. This was standard Communist rhetoric in reply to Western discussion, but the Soviet military measures that Khrushchev announced on July 8 were carefully presented as countermeasures to military *actions* by the West.

Khrushchev referred to Kennedy's proposal to increase the defense budget by $3.5 billion over the amount contained in Eisenhower's draft budget, an increase of about 7.5 per cent. He mentioned also an 18 per cent increase in the defense budget of the Federal Republic for 1961 and spoke of "the considerable growth in military spending in Britain, France, and the NATO countries." Then he concluded dramatically:

Taking into account the obtaining situation, the Soviet Government was compelled to instruct the Defense Ministry to suspend, temporarily, pending special orders, the reduction of the armed forces planned for 1961.

In view of the growing military budgets in the NATO countries, the Soviet Government has passed a decision to increase defense spendings in the current year by 3,144,000,000 rubles, thereby raising the total military spending in 1961 to 12,399,000,000 rubles.[29]

This constituted an increase of 26 per cent of the announced expenditures for defense.

Why did Khrushchev launch his new political offensive against the positions of the Western powers in Europe? It is true that his earlier claims, demands, and threats had never been allowed to lapse, but he had relaxed the pressure on the West after the U-2 incident in May, 1960. He had declared in East Berlin that the conditions for winning the coveted prize of West Berlin and Germany from the West had long since been "ripe," but that these conditions would "ripen" better as more time passed. What made him think that in the spring of 1961 the time had come for the harvest?

We may dismiss at the outset the notion that Khrushchev was compelled to resume his attack in June, 1961, by economic or political difficulties in the Soviet Union or in the satellite empire. Although it is perfectly true that Khrushchev and, to a greater extent, Ulbricht face such difficulties, the former cannot afford to disregard the more important risks he incurs by renewing his political offensive against the three major Western powers. Similarly, it is quite improbable, some speculations to the contrary notwithstanding, that Khrushchev renewed his pressure on the West in order to be able to prove to the Chinese Communists at the Twenty-second Party Congress, in October, that successful political aggression can be combined with his declared policy of coexistence. It would be quite adventurous for a Communist leader to let his policy be dominated by Communist rivalries when the first requirement for correct action is an accurate assessment of enemy strengths and weaknesses so as neither to miss opportunities for success nor to underrate the risks and costs of failure.

Finally, it is absurd to assume that Khrushchev resumed his political aggression in the spring of 1961 because of any political speeches in West Germany or because of improvements in West German defense. The Soviet Union, of course, is interested in weakening Western military power, but it would be insulting Khrushchev's intelligence to believe that he is frightened by the Federal Republic. Years ago, he publicly declared that he could turn West Germany into a "cemetery" at will. Khrushchev's tirades against Germany's military contributions to the NATO alliance and against German speeches dealing with the German territory that fell under Communist domination at the end of World War II serve only to arouse latent anti-German feelings in the West. These tirades are propagandistic justifications of Soviet policy, not a disclosure of its motives or an explanation of its timing.

The true reasons for Khrushchev's renewed political

attack on Berlin and Germany must lie in his estimate of the state of the political and military global balance of power. A shift in that balance favorable to the Soviet Union can occur in three ways: (1) by a dwindling of Western power or by failures of Western policies, (2) by gains in Communist strength, especially in the form of military power, and (3) by political developments in the rest of the world that are not necessarily directly controlled or instigated by either side but can be exploited by the Communists. It is likely that Khrushchev regarded the spring of 1961 as an auspicious time for new ventures against the West in Europe because of favorable developments in all three respects.

At the time of the Vienna meetings, the United States had suffered setbacks in Laos and Cuba. Khrushchev had not hesitated to assist Castro by addressing rocket threats to the U.S. Government. In the past, such threats had been reserved for lesser powers. Furthermore, Khrushchev believed that the emergence of new states in Asia and Africa had weakened the global position of the West and would weaken it more in the future, if Western intervention in "wars of liberation" could be prevented. Khrushchev had been angered by United Nations activities in the Congo. From his performance at the United Nations General Assembly in the autumn of 1960, it was clear that in his view the United Nations had functioned in the Congo as a political instrument of the "imperialistic powers." Whereupon, he advocated the "troika principle," which would give equal veto power in international executive agencies to the Western nations, the socialist countries, and the new states. In Vienna, Khrushchev reaffirmed this troika principle specifically to the staffing of the executive agency that would control an agreement to ban nuclear tests. As the *aide-mémoire* "On Arms and Nuclear Tests" pointed out, with distinctive allusion to Hammarskjöld, "It is well known that while there are neutral states, there are not, nor can there be, neutral men." [30]

In this way, Khrushchev also informed Kennedy that he was not interested in the progress of the arms-control negotiations at Geneva and that the time had passed for any Western effort to attain a tolerable compromise on Berlin and Germany by compensatory Western concessions in negotiations on arms control or disarmament. Perhaps Khrushchev had learned a lesson in the weeks that preceded the abortive summit conference in Paris in May, 1960, when both Herter and Dillon had linked the issue of Berlin with that of arms control in order to induce Khrushchev to be more reasonable.

It is possible that neither the setbacks of American foreign policy nor Communist estimates of the consequences of decolonialization alone were sufficient to account for Khrushchev's resumption of his political offensive in Europe. In particular, the Kremlin must have considered the possibility that the events in Laos and Cuba would cause Kennedy to redouble efforts to resist a political defeat in Europe. Certainly, the President went to Vienna with the intention of leaving precisely this impression on Khrushchev's mind. In these circumstances, estimates of the military balance between the East and the West and its bearing on the German and Berlin issues must have been of particularly great importance.

Perhaps Khrushchev believed that no improvement in NATO defense and no changes in NATO strategy could be made in time for a Western attempt to counter the execution of his political threat by conventional military means. Perhaps he believed further that in such circumstances, the risk of nuclear war over Berlin would appear so grave to the "sane" people in the West that the "madmen" would finally be constrained to yield to political pressure rather than risk World War III over the future of Germany and Berlin. If this was his belief, it would be good strategy from his point of view to stimulate Western fear of nuclear war in order to benefit from its political consequences. A German observer remarked correctly:

The military aspect is only one aspect of the crisis over Berlin. If it is overemphasized, it can lead to a kind of hysteria which saps [Western] staying power.[31]

143

The most ominous interpretation of the Soviet policy, however, is that Khrushchev believes that the Soviet military position relative to that of the United States has so improved within the last year that he can afford to intensify his military threats, should Western political resistance prove to be unflinching. In this case, more dramatic developments might still occur. For example, Khrushchev would have to resort to entirely new methods of trying to convince the West that the Soviet Union has greater ICBM capabilities than it is credited with in the West. A mere repetition of verbal boasts would probably not be enough.

In June and July, 1961, however, Khrushchev carefully confined himself to public claims of strategic-weapons *equality*. There was no real evidence that he was unwilling to resume *negotiations* with the Western governments, perhaps at the point where he hoped to begin them at the summit conference in Paris in 1960, that is, approximately at the point where the Geneva Foreign Ministers' Conference had ended. In any event, he could sit back waiting for signs of fear, disunity, and weakness in the West.

15

The Counterattack

THE U.S. REPLY to the Soviet *aide-mémoire* of June 4 was not presented to the Kremlin until July 17, 1961.[1] In certain respects, the note was firmer than a number of earlier Western diplomatic communications during the long conflict.

The note said that were it not for the Communist demands, there would be "no reason for a crisis over Berlin." It was these demands that endangered peace. They were without legal foundation, were made in disregard of solemn international commitments on the part of the Soviet Union, and violated the interests of the NATO countries. The note repeatedly warned that any unilateral move by the Soviet Government in its German policy could be interpreted by the NATO countries "as a purposeful threat to their national security." Soviet foreign policy might have "unforeseeable consequences."

Since "the grave dangers" of the situation were associated with the threat of *unilateral* Soviet action, the road to negotiations was not barred. In fact, special care was taken to point out that the road was open. Perhaps the sentence in the U.S. note most relevant in this regard was the following:

> That the United States is not wedded to any particular arrangement for Berlin is demonstrated by the all-Berlin solution which was proposed at Geneva in 1959. It has accepted the possibility of practical arrangements intended to improve the present situation in Berlin until such time as an over-all solution of the German problem can be achieved.

The American note also recalled the Western peace plan of May 14, 1959, as evidence of U.S. interest in negotiations affecting the future of Germany.

Since the Soviet *aide-mémoire* of June 4 had also indicated a Communist interest in negotiation, the two main purposes of the American note were to make it clear to the Soviet Government that while the United States was ready to enter negotiations, it would not do so under duress, and to state with a degree of firmness equaling that of the Soviet *aide-mémoire* that the Communist aims were legally unjustified and unacceptable to the United States.

The U.S. note again insisted on the legal rights of the Western powers to remain in Berlin.[2] But special care was taken to point out that these rights were important in order to safeguard the freedom of the Berliners rather than to perpetuate the occupation regime. It is possible that this particular emphasis was chosen in deference to British views of the issue. The British were known to be apprehensive—and perhaps not incorrectly so—that in the event of war, the protection of Western occupation rights would not constitute a cause strong enough to rally the British people and the free world generally behind a Western war effort. The protection of the freedom of the West Berliners evidently would be a more compelling cause than any legal argument, however sound. The British position had been succinctly stated by Edward Heath, Lord Privy Seal, in Commons on March 17, 1961:

> The Western powers are in Berlin not just to maintain an outdated occupation. They are there to fulfill their responsibilities toward the people of the city.[3]

The issues singled out for attack in the American note included those the Soviet *aide-mémoire* had tried to obscure, especially with regard to the foreign policy of the Federal Republic and to the status of East Berlin. Soviet allegations that West Germany was contemplating the use of force to achieve reunification, and that her defense measures were a menace to peace, were rejected in considerable detail. It was pointed out that the West German forces were "fully integrated in NATO."

> The Federal Republic does not seek, or intend to develop, an independent nuclear capability or the transfer of nuclear weapons to its national jurisdiction.

The most aggressive language politically was used in those passages that dealt with the status of East Berlin:

> It is significant that the Soviet Union having previously occupied East Berlin and violated its four power status by establishing there an alleged "G.D.R." government, now proposes that its troops will be stationed in a "free city" of West Berlin. The Soviet government would thus seek to extend its post-war empire by the absorption of the eastern sector of Berlin and to shift the four-power principle from all of Berlin to the western part of the city alone.

Probably because of differences of opinion within the Western alliance on the border issue, the question of boundaries was not directly discussed in the note. Khrushchev had boldly declared that it was no longer an issue at all; the present borders could not be changed. All that remained was to put the seal on the

Potsdam Agreement by a peace treaty that would give legal sanction to the temporary lines marking the eastern boundaries of the Soviet Zone. Instead of meeting this assault head-on, the U.S. note reminded the Soviet Government that the Potsdam Agreement of 1945 referred to "the preparation of a peace settlement for Germany to be accepted by the government of Germany when a government adequate for the purpose is established." This was, in fact, restating not only that reunification would have to precede the peace settlement with Germany, but also that no unilateral peace treaty "with the part of Germany's territory termed 'German Democratic Republic' by the Soviet Government" could turn the existing lines of demarcation into legally recognized borders. According to the Western position, which was restated in the note, such a unilateral treaty "could have no validity in international law" nor "affect in any way whatsoever the rights of the Western powers." Thus, the U.S. note at least implied that the German borders would have to be established legally by four-power negotiations, even if the existing, temporary lines of demarcation were recognized rather than changed.

If the Soviet Government reads this implication into the passages of the U.S. note that deal with the Potsdam Agreement, Khrushchev may well refuse to negotiate, or temporarily feign such a refusal, and increase the pressure on the West in the expectation that a deepening of the crisis will eventually demoralize the Western governments. But the Western powers also have untapped political resources. For example, in a television interview on July 23, 1961, Secretary Rusk explained that should the crisis reach a point of very high tension, the issue might be taken to the United Nations. While it was to be expected, he said, that a Western proposal for airing the conflict would run into a Soviet veto in the Security Council, the United States "would not be at all nervous about putting these issues to the General Assembly" and there "engage the consciousness of the world." [4] The observation that the U.S. Government would take such a step without nervousness was not necessarily an indication of self-confidence, but the Secretary said that he believed a discussion in the General Assembly would at least discredit Khrushchev among the neutral and uncommitted nations, where he had "some ambitions." [5]

In order not to get lost in the details of diplomatic moves and countermoves, it is useful to compare the Western reaction to the Soviet political offensive in 1959 with that of 1961. The main difference lies not in the arguments advanced by the Western governments but in the measures that were taken to back them up. President Eisenhower did not resort to any specific military measures to increase the credibility of U.S. policy on Berlin and Germany. By contrast, President Kennedy attempted to make the Soviet Government and the people in the Western countries realize that specific American defense measures and a strengthening of NATO's defenses in Europe were necessary to meet Soviet Cold War aggression and the renewed Soviet political offensive on the Western positions in Europe in particular.

Meanwhile, both the Soviet Government and its stooges in the G.D.R. used every trick to probe the depth of Western resolution. For example, immediately after the Vienna meeting, the Soviet campaign against the "provocations" of any Bundestag meetings in West Berlin was renewed. The Geneva negotiations on the cessation of nuclear tests came to a standstill. Ulbricht predicted that he would have control of civilian air traffic in Berlin as of August 1, 1961. Even the conference on political settlement of the war in Laos—the only issue on which Kennedy and Khrushchev had agreed in Vienna—made no visible progress. When the West German note of July 12 was given to Gromyko in Moscow, he feigned anger and remarked to the German Ambassador that on the day the separate treaty would be signed, Soviet troops would be massed along the border of West Germany. Ambassador Menshikov indicated at a Washington cocktail party that he believed that the Western powers were only bluffing. Prior to President Kennedy's speech of July 25, 1961, it was reported that Communist diplomats in the West were anxious to find out whether there was any strength behind the firm statements made by Western statesmen.

The American note was reinforced by the similarly firm replies of the British and French governments. Any doubts that the U.S. note meant what it said were dispelled by the far-reaching defense measures that President Kennedy announced on July 25.[6] While these measures were designed to meet Communist aggression wherever it might occur, the Soviet threat to Berlin and Germany provided an immediate rationale for them. The President prefaced his announcement with another energetic and eloquent declaration of American resolution to honor U.S. commitments in West Berlin, if need be, by force:

> I hear it said that West Berlin is untenable. So was Bastogne. So, in fact, was Stalingrad. Any dangerous spot is tenable if brave men will make it so. We do not want to fight—but we have fought before.[7]

No other Western statement in the long history of the crisis had been firmer.

Kennedy explained that the new defense preparations were part of the long-term buildup of American strength that had been under way since January, 1961. The measures were "based on our needs," he declared, "to meet a world-wide threat." They were in addition to those financed by the supplementary defense allocations requested by the President from Congress in March,

1961, which Khrushchev had used in his speech of July 8 to justify the increase in the Soviet military budget. Kennedy's announcement thus was the third step in a new arms race precipitated by Khrushchev's policy. Kennedy preceded his announcement of the magnitude of the new defense budget by declaring that "in the days and months ahead, I shall not hesitate to ask for additional measures from the Congress or exercise any of the executive powers I possess to meet this threat to peace."

The President announced that the following day he would request from Congress additional appropriations totaling $3.5 billion. More than half this amount, $1.8 billion, would be used for procuring non-nuclear weapons, ammunition, and equipment. The remainder would be spent for: (1) an increase in the Army of 125,000 men to bring its total strength up to one million men; (2) an increase of 29,000 men in the Navy and 63,000 men in the Air Force; (3) an increase in the airlift capacity of the United States by activating a number of Air Transport squadrons and tactical squadrons of the Air National Guard; (4) an increase in the airlift, sealift, and antisubmarine capacity of the Navy by retaining ships and planes scheduled for retirement and reactivating others; and (5) a delay in the deactivation of B-47 bombers. Finally, the President asked that $207 million be spent on civil defense. Although this amount constituted only 6 per cent of the total request for additional funds, it was an effective reminder to the American people that the struggle across the oceans with Communism affected their lives at home, and that the national security requires not only financial and personal sacrifices but also involves their physical safety. In the Kremlin, Kennedy's announcements of July 25 undoubtedly gave rise to a new evaluation of whether West Berlin, the "sovereignty" of the German Democratic Republic, the legalization of the existing boundaries in Europe, and the hope of destroying NATO were worth an accelerated arms race with the United States. The men in the Kremlin must also have considered the time it would take for the new American buildup of strength to have an effect on a resolution of the Berlin issue by force of arms, should it come to that, and on the outcome of East-West conflicts elsewhere in the world. Whatever conclusion they drew, they must have realized that in the third year of their political offensive in Europe, one of the risks that had attended their ventures from the beginning had suddenly increased very sharply. Did all this not call for an even more general reconsideration of Soviet policy? Could Khrushchev in these circumstances hope to continue to make gains in the Cold War under the cloak of professions that he favored peace and coexistence?

In July, 1961, yet another hazard attending Soviet policy became apparent. It appeared that the risks

Khrushchev was incurring by his political offensive in Europe did not lie exclusively in increasing American determination to resist Soviet demands in the strengthening of NATO solidarity, or in the military measures that he was inducing the United States to take. The Germans living in the Soviet Zone were deeply disturbed by Khrushchev's policy and Ulbricht's statements of its implications. The stream of refugees arriving in West Berlin from the Soviet Zone rose alarmingly in July, and there were signs that unrest was growing among the Germans who stayed behind. Perhaps neither Khrushchev nor Ulbricht had taken full account of the dangers of these developments.

The flight from the Soviet Zone amounted to a silent plebiscite in which Ulbricht's and Khrushchev's policies were rejected. In the first six months of 1960, 88,500 Germans had left the Soviet Zone. The corresponding figure for 1961 was 103,000. Possibly the increase for this period may be attributed in large part to growing dissatisfaction with the widespread economic disorganization in the Soviet Zone. There was a serious shortage of industrial and consumer goods and of foodstuffs. Economic planning had failed; the morale of workers, engineers, and plant managers was low.[8] But the steep rise in the flood of refugees in the month of July was undoubtedly also caused by fear that the gateway to freedom would be closed forever, if Khrushchev and Ulbricht succeeded in turning West Berlin into a

155

"Free City." During the first half of July, 12,000 new refugees came to the West Berlin reception centers, and between July 9 and July 16, no less than 8,000 new arrivals were counted. This meant more than 1,000 arrivals a day, a figure not exceeded in any previous July. It is estimated that even these figures fell from 15 to 20 per cent short of the actual number, since many refugees find a haven in West Berlin with relatives and friends or leave the city by airplane at their own expense, and are not included in the count at the reception centers. "One cannot help drawing a parallel with the situation in May, 1953," Otto Frei observed, "when more than 1,000 refugees a day used to arrive in West Berlin." [9] (In 1953, there were uprisings in the German Democratic Republic against the Communist regime.)

The refugees who turned their backs on Communism included many young people, "who had been trained at the expense of the 'G.D.R.' Communist schools and institutions." [10] In addition, the defections aggravated problems of the zonal economy at a time of severe crisis. The mass exodus was incontrovertible proof to the world that Ulbricht's policies and propaganda had been unsuccessful.

Other signs of unrest in the Soviet Zone were potentially even more important to the outcome of the struggle between the East and the West than the mass migration to the Western Zone.

Close reading of the controlled press in the German Democratic Republic suggested that popular dissatisfaction with Khrushchev's policies was no isolated phenomenon and that Communist authorities felt it necessary to permit its public expression.

In a discussion among workers in Halle, reported in the city newspaper *Freiheit,* embarrassing questions were asked. Should not reunification precede a peace treaty? Why was it impossible to hold free elections? In *Leipziger Volkszeitung,* a worker demanded that the borders should be opened for the free travel of Germans from east to west and from west to east. Residents of Wismar asked for a change in the abnormal situation in the whole of Berlin, not just a Communist "solution of the West Berlin problem." In Gera, a Party secretary wrote in *Volkswacht* that the population of the Soviet Zone was not convinced of the necessity of a separate peace treaty. The Magdeburg paper *Volksstimme* published a statement of a reader to the effect that the Soviet draft of a peace treaty with Germany did not serve peace, for the treaty "would bar the road to a life of freedom for the German people forever." [11] It was also reported that the East German student paper *Forum* criticized the German policy of the Soviet Government.[12] And East Berlin construction workers, who had led the 1953 revolt against Ulbricht, warned Khrushchev to "have no illusions"; they would not permit him to take over West Berlin.[13]

It is difficult to estimate correctly the momentum of all the developments in the Soviet Zone and their impact on the outcome of the conflict over the divided city. Such developments are not fully under the control of the main protagonists in the struggle, but constitute the reaction of those whose conditions of life are most immediately affected by it. If Khrushchev's decision to resume his political offensive in Vienna was not determined by the grave political and economic difficulties that his functionary Ulbricht faces in the Soviet Zone, it is possible that a popular revolt in the German Democratic Republic against the Communist regime would force Khrushchev either to relent in his pressure on the West or to resort to violence. He might ruthlessly suppress any uprising, as he did twice before, eight years ago in Germany and five years ago in Hungary. In that event, he would surely try to justify such military intervention by holding West Berlin, the Federal Republic, and other Western powers responsible for the results of his own policy. He might not only sign the separate peace treaty with the German Democratic Republic but go further and attempt to force the immediate absorption of West Berlin in the Communist realm. This would bring the crisis to a new climax and would make the avoidance of war considerably more difficult. But Khrushchev himself must be aware of the fact that in view of the intense, political participation of the Western powers in the struggle for

Berlin since November, 1958, the resort to violence against a revolt in the German Democratic Republic would be a far more dangerous enterprise than was his intervention in Hungary in 1956.

For this reason, he might be careful to leave the control and suppression of any popular uprising in the Soviet Zone to Ulbricht and his police forces, and mask any Soviet participation in it, as long as such a policy promised to be successful. It is even possible that Khrushchev may sacrifice Ulbricht, if he believes that his anti-Western policy can otherwise make no headway.

16

Conclusions

THE ALLIED GOVERNMENTS have neither yielded to the pressure of missile diplomacy nor refused to negotiate with the Soviet Government. Protesting that their rights in Berlin could not be abrogated by unilateral action, insisting that the ultimatum be rescinded, and refusing to negotiate under the threat of unilateral action, the Western powers have steered a course of moderation. Under the Eisenhower Administration, the United States tried not to aggravate the crisis by defense measures, for example, by redeploying or alerting military forces or by an increase in their armaments. The only exception was the seven-hour alert at the time of the Paris Conference in May, 1960. In 1961, however, two increases in the U.S. defense budget were announced. Efforts were also made to change the size and structure of the NATO forces and thus, at least by implication, NATO strategy. The second increase in the U.S. defense budget, in June, 1961, occurred after Khrushchev had renewed his political offensive in the spring. Although Kennedy's decision was not dictated by this fact alone, his action lent credibility to the Western resolution to resist Khrushchev's new political attack in Europe.

Until the end of 1960, the nonverbal measures in defense of Berlin were local and economic in character; most of them were taken to keep West Berlin economically stable and to strengthen the ability of the city to withstand another blockade. According to Mayor Brandt, enough goods have been stored in Berlin for the city to hold out for a year, if it should be cut off from West Germany. The morale of the Berliners—a critical factor in the crisis—has not been impaired. It is likely to remain high, as long as the Western powers do not compromise their basic interests in Berlin. In the Cold War by proxy, economic measures brought to bear upon the Ulbricht regime by the Federal Government in the autumn of 1960 proved to be especially effective.

While the cohesion of the Western allies has been put under additional strain by the Communist threat to Berlin, and while British–West German relations, in particular, have suffered occasionally in consequence of

161

Soviet diplomacy and propaganda, these setbacks have been neither irreversible nor serious enough to enable the Soviet Government to have its will. The outcome of the crisis depends primarily on the political and military stance of the United States, the leading power in the Western alliance.

The Western powers, as well as the Communists, realize that the outcome of the conflict will affect both the freedom of 2.2 million people in West Berlin and the position of the United States in Germany and Europe. Indeed, the future status of West Berlin involves not only the future of NATO and the confidence of our allies in the power and resolution of the United States, but also the hopes and expectations in countries that are uncommitted in the East-West struggle or ruled by Communist governments. The Berlin crisis is a global issue.

The Western powers have gained time, since the deadline set by the original ultimatum passed without irreparable consequences, if not uneventfully; Western occupation troops have been neither withdrawn from Berlin nor reduced in strength. The so-called German Democratic Republic has not been recognized, and the Western idea that the peaceful reunification of the divided country must precede the conclusion of a peace treaty with Germany still is basic policy.

Until the end of 1960, the Western powers held their position by diplomatic action. The reasons for their policy, which the preceding account has suggested, can be listed as follows:

1. The exposed geographical position of West Berlin.
2. The risk of local war associated with any offensive strategy on the part of the West.
3. The risk of any local war developing into general war.
4. The discrepancy between the seemingly narrow scope of the issue and the frightful nature of nuclear war—the possible (however remotely) result of failure to resolve the conflict by negotiation.
5. The general preference for deterring the expansion of Communist power to forcing its contraction.
6. The associated belief in the wickedness of political expansionism.
7. Specifically, the defensive character of NATO.
8. The difficulty of reaching policy agreement among members of a coalition on offensive measures, which is even greater than that of reaching agreement on common defense.
9. The overtly nonviolent character of the Soviet threat.
10. The encouragement of peaceful, negotiatory tactics by Soviet denials that they had meant to confront the West with an ultimatum on Berlin.
11. The belief in the moral and legal rights to the Western presence in Berlin.

12. The hope that this belief, if forcefully voiced, would induce the Communists to relent in their denial of the validity of these rights.

13. The belief that Khrushchev's protestations of his interest in competitive coexistence may offer opportunities to the West for persuading him to assent to a mutually acceptable settlement of the issue.

14. The belief that Western concessions may yet lead to Communist counterconcessions.

15. The belief that a new negotiated settlement of the Berlin issue would be preferable to the old agreements, since the former would be agreed to by the Soviet Government, while it challenges the latter.

16. The belief that a new "interim" settlement would be preferable to the old agreements, because it would buy time and lower the pressure on the West at least for a while.

In 1961, many of these reasons have remained valid, but the crisis has been aggravated by Khrushchev. This fact, along with the setbacks of American foreign policy in Southeast Asia and Cuba, have if anything stiffened American resistance to Communist political pressure in Europe.

In trying to resolve an international conflict by nonviolent means, diplomacy can always follow any one of three general courses of action. First, it can counter the proposals of the adversary by *counterproposals* in the hope of negotiating a mutually acceptable compromise on the issue that has been raised by him. This tactic may or may not result in some net loss. If a net loss results, it is likely to be smaller than the gain that the opponent originally attempted to make. If the defensive power takes no loss in the end, this may be a consequence of the fact that its counterproposals embodied not only certain concessions to the opponent's original demands, but also new counterdemands, some or all of which the opponent saw fit to meet. Indeed, it may happen that both parties will make, or believe they have made, gains in the final bargain.

The so-called interim solution of the Berlin issue, offered by the Western powers in Geneva on July 28, 1959, was clearly a proposal that countered the original Soviet ultimatum, and it was confined to Berlin. West German criticism of this plan was predicated on the judgment that its acceptance by the Soviet Government would have resulted in too heavy a loss to the West. By the same token, the rejection of the plan by Gromyko was an ominous sign that the Soviet Government regarded that loss as too low from its viewpoint. Similarly, Soviet intimations in the spring of 1960 that further negotiations of an interim settlement on the basis of the rejected Western proposal would be possible at the summit meeting in Paris seemed to support the Western critics who said that toward the close of the Geneva Conference, the West offered too much to the East.

In its *aide-mémoire* of February 17, 1961, presented to the Federal Government, the Kremlin suggested once more that an interim solution could be found for the status of West Berlin. Also in Vienna, it became clear that Soviet policy had not been altered. Khrushchev merely tried to give the impression that he would obtain in 1961 what he had failed to gain in the two preceding years.

Nor did any of the three Western powers have occasion, until the end of July, 1961, to present or disclose any new counterproposals that might be negotiated. The U.S. note of July 18 merely referred back to earlier Western plans that had been presented to, and rejected by, the Soviet Government in 1959. After Kennedy's meeting in Vienna, it became necessary to convince the Soviet Government that the solidarity and firmness of the Western powers had been strengthened rather than weakened by Khrushchev's new political assault. The President was concerned that Khrushchev might misjudge Western intentions; "in the thermo-nuclear age, any misjudgment on either side about the intentions of the other could rain more devastation in several hours than has been wrought in all the wars of human history." [1] A new and forceful rebuff of Khrushchev's renewed threat seemed, therefore, more important to the President than the public advancing of counterproposals, which Khrushchev might have interpreted as a sign that his new political offensive was succeeding.

Conclusions

In the same speech in which the President announced the second increase in 1961 of the U.S. defense budget, however, he hinted in very general language at those aspects of the moot issue on which negotiations would be possible. First, he said that the United States had previously shown its "readiness" to remove any actual irritants in West Berlin." [2] This may have referred to an item of the Western compromise proposal, presented in Geneva at the end of July, 1959, according to which propaganda and intelligence activities in Berlin were to be curbed. Second, the President recognized the Soviet Union's "historical concerns about their security in central and eastern Europe" and stated his belief that "arrangements can be worked out which will help to meet those concerns." [3] This statement was so broad that it did not even preclude negotiations on disengagement or conceivably Western willingness to include provisions in the peace treaty with an all-German government that would prescribe the military and political status of reunified Germany. Such a provision would, of course, constitute a major concession to the Soviet Union and a radical departure from the stand Adenauer and the three major Western powers have taken in the past.

Interestingly enough, a suggestion that just such a counterproposal could be made to the Soviet Government had unexpectedly come from the German Bundestag at the end of June. On June 30, Eugen Gerstenmaier, the President of the West German Parliament, had presented a declaration on the German problem that included this point.[4]

The second course of action by which diplomacy can resolve an international conflict with nonviolent means is to try to *enlarge the issue* raised by the opponent by relating it to connected issues. This tactic is advantageous, if it permits a restatement of the original issue in new terms. The Western powers adopted this tactic in their initial replies to the Soviet ultimatum, and more specifically at the beginning of the Geneva Conference, by proposing the "package plan." This plan was to deal with the Berlin issue by embedding it in the larger one of German unification. In the face of the original Soviet threat, the package plan tried to uphold the Western policy of German reunification. This attempt to seize the initiative in the negotiations failed because the Soviet Government had already countered it, as was to be expected, by its own proposal that peace be concluded first and unification be left to negotiations between the two German governments.

The sensitivity of the Soviet Government to all Western attempts to enlarge the issue could again be gauged at Khrushchev's press conference at Jakarta, when he rejected, with extraordinary promptness, Herter's plan for a plebiscite to be held under international control in both parts of Germany. The plebiscite was to give *the*

Germans an opportunity to voice their preference either for the Eastern peace plan or for the Western proposals on Germany. Khrushchev rejected this idea because in his view it represented intervention in the internal affairs of the German people.

As its third course, diplomacy can try in two ways to *enlarge the arena of conflict*. It can make its willingness to meet *other* known interests of the opponent dependent on his relenting his pressure on the issue he has originally raised, or it can seize the initiative by introducing counterpressures on entirely new issues. Various illustrations of the first (the defensive) way of enlarging the arena of conflict can be found in the record to date of the East-West struggle over the future of Berlin and Germany. For example, in 1959, the United States delayed agreement to the holding of a summit conference and to Khrushchev's visit to this country in order to compel the Soviet Government to conduct itself with more restraint in the crisis. Since it was Khrushchev's wish to come to the United States and to attend another summit meeting, U.S. diplomacy could utilize threats of refusal to meet that wish for influencing the course of negotiations at Geneva. At the meeting at Camp David, Eisenhower did not enlarge the arena of conflict, but agreed to negotiations at the summit, under the conditions that no further ultimatum would be issued and no unilateral action would be taken or threatened by the Soviet Government. Khrushchev was willing to change his tactics accordingly, but this change was temporary and involved only the means, and not the ends, of his policy. After the meeting at Camp David, it was primarily De Gaulle's achievement that the date of the summit conference was delayed until May, 1960. The West gained more time.

Just prior to the summit conference in Paris, Herter and Dillon tried to enlarge the arena of the impending negotiations by raising issues of arms control in the context of their discussions of Berlin's and Germany's future. They stated explicitly that any progress toward reaching agreement on arms control, in which the Soviet Union was presumed to be interested at that time, would depend on the Soviet Government's showing restraint in its German policy.

At the meeting in Vienna early in June, 1961, Khrushchev indicated to President Kennedy that he was no longer interested in reaching agreement on the cessation of nuclear tests, unless the troika principle was applied to the control agencies to be set up. He thereby served notice that he would not permit the Western governments to halt his new political offensive in Europe by a refusal to meet him halfway on other issues. In effect, Khrushchev proclaimed that the Soviet Union had no interest in reaching a compromise with the Western powers on *any* major political issue; it was

170

this blunt disclosure of general hostility, rather than merely the resumption of the political offensive in Europe, through which Khrushchev heightened international tension and aggravated the Berlin crisis.

The second (*the aggressive*) way of enlarging the arena of conflict is even more difficult to follow than are merely *defensive* efforts to that effect. Since the Western powers are essentially peaceful and preoccupied with deterring Communist expansion, they cannot easily free themselves of the belief that it is always morally preferable and politically prudent to limit political conflict. They do not believe that enlarging the arena of conflict may, in certain circumstances, lead to a more stable peace.

In the history of the Berlin crisis, the most outstanding example of an enlargement of the arena of conflict by the West is the U-2 incident. It did not occur by Western design. It was therefore Eisenhower's and Herter's endorsement of the espionage activity, after the incident had occurred, rather than the incident itself, that enlarged the arena of conflict. It appears that this episode, whatever may be said about its moral and legal implications, assisted the Western powers in halting Khrushchev's political advance in Europe.

President Kennedy's efforts to alter the size and composition of U.S. and NATO forces may not only improve the military capabilities of the West for meeting

171

future Communist military aggression by proxy, whether in Asia, the Middle East, or in Europe, but may also increase Western opportunities for seizing the political initiative. Success in the Cold War with Communism depends on the ability to exploit the political value of arms.

Postscript

During July and early August, 1961, Khrushchev gave the impression that he sensed the danger of losing not only the initiative in the conflict over the future of Germany but also full control over the risks incurred by his policy. The United States had provided tangible proof that to avoid further political setbacks, possibly even an act of political surrender in Western Europe, it was willing to pay the price of a limited arms race with the Soviet Union. The solidarity of the three major Western powers was not shaken, and the stream of refugees from the Soviet Zone increased from day to day.

Khrushchev may not have believed that the Western countermeasures would change the local strategic situation in time to affect the struggle for Berlin, but it is unlikely that he viewed with equanimity the consequences of an accelerated arms race on the economy of the Soviet Union and on the prospects of Soviet foreign policy in the longer run. He felt it necessary to marshal new arguments to justify his insistence that a peace treaty with the German Democratic Republic be signed in 1961, and it appears that Western countermeasures created doubts in the Communist camp that Soviet policy had been kept within the bounds of safety.

The main risk was that the political conflict over the future of Berlin and Germany might erupt into war. Khrushchev tried to reduce this risk by a barrage of new warnings and threats aimed at augmenting the fear of war in the West. Even though the risk of war was less than Khrushchev claimed, such warnings were useful to the Soviet Government, which has always used military threats and warnings of war to inhibit and restrict the enemy in his political moves.

Early in July, while attending a performance at the Bolshoi Theater in Moscow, Khrushchev had discussed the crisis with Sir Frank Roberts, the British Ambassador, in ominous language. It was reported that the Soviet leader not only had said that the division of Germany should continue but also had asked Sir Frank: "Why should 200 million people die because of 2 million Berliners?" [1] In connection with the French plan to transfer a division from Algeria to Europe, he was reported to have commented that he could mobilize 300 divisions. Khrushchev also mentioned that he would need only twenty bombs to destroy France and Great Britain.[2]

In August, Khrushchev made a number of similar public statements. In his radio and television speech of August 7, 1961, he tried to convince his listeners that it was President Kennedy who had resorted to threats and had presented the Soviet Government with an ultimatum. The Soviet leader observed that military hysteria was intentionally being created in the United States and that the danger of all-out nuclear war had greatly increased. He played upon the old Soviet theme that it would never be possible for "the two giants"— the Soviet Union and the United States—to fight a limited war against each other; neither side would ever be ready to admit defeat without having used all the weapons at its disposal. War would come not only to the homes of the American people but would rage with destructive fury in all the countries that were allied with the United States.

Khrushchev again dwelt at length on the possibility that "an act of madness" by people "possessed by suicidal mania" might unleash World War III. He reverted to his preoccupation with self-control (that is, self-control by the enemy) as a prerequisite for the rational conduct of international affairs. Recalling an incident from World War II, when a desperate Soviet General had committed suicide before his eyes, Khrushchev said:

> I do not want to draw a direct analogy, but in the West there are some people who are losing self-possession and self-control. In the story I have just told, it was one man who perished. But in present conditions, if some Western leaders would act recklessly and push the world to a new war, such a suicidal act would spell death to millions and millions of people.[3]

In its emotional overtones, this statement strongly resembled Khrushchev's remarks at his press conference after the breakdown of the Paris summit meeting in May, 1960, when he commented on the alert status of American forces that Secretary Gates had then ordered. Khrushchev is well aware of the fact that he cannot win the war of nerves if the Western statesmen are "mad" enough to change it into a shooting war or if they lack the "sanity" to yield to his demands.

While trying to evoke the specter of nuclear war as a consequence of Western intransigence, Khrushchev continued to temper his ominous fantasies by reassurances that everything could be settled rationally at the conference table. He made remarks to that effect on various occasions, for example, on the occasion of Italian Premier Fanfani's visit to Moscow, and at a reception for a visiting Rumanian delegation. He expressed his belief that there would not be a war over Berlin [4] and welcomed President Kennedy's expression of hope for a peaceful settlement.

At the same time, the Soviet leader advanced two interesting new reasons for urgent unilateral Soviet action on the peace treaty if four-power agreement could not be reached. In his speech of August 7, 1961, he raised, and immediately answered, the question of why it was "necessary" to sign a peace treaty with Germany at this time. He treated this subject in the form of a dialogue with an imaginary interrogator, a stylistic device that is especially well known from Stalin's speeches and always leaves the listener at a loss to decide whether he is witnessing the resolution of the dictator's inner doubts, the reflection of discussions that the speaker has actually had with lesser members of the Communist elite, or an attempt to anticipate and to silence criticism; in the absence of free public discussion, the intent of public, dictatorial rhetoric is mysterious. Khrushchev exclaimed: *"Someone might say,* however: Is it as necessary as all that to sign a peace treaty with Germany now? Why not wait another two or three years or even more for the conclusion of this treaty? Perhaps that would eliminate tension, *remove the danger of war?"* [5] (Italics added.)

Of course, Khrushchev replied in the negative, but for a reason that deserves special attention: "If we renounced the conclusion of a peace treaty, they [the Western powers] would regard this as a strategic breakthrough and would widen the range of their demands at once." [6]

Khrushchev amplified this remarkable statement by saying that the Western powers would first insist on the liquidation of the socialist system in the Soviet Zone, next try to annex the territories "restored" to Poland and Czechoslovakia under the Potsdam Agreement, and finally abolish socialism in all countries of the Soviet camp. This exposition of a dangerous "strategic breakthrough" by the enemy and the avalanche fantasies produced by thoughts of political compromise are interesting not only because they reveal Khrushchev's view of international conflict, but also because they allude to the possibility that Western recognition of the German Democratic Republic, or possibly its borders, might induce him to renounce the conclusion of a peace treaty.

Khrushchev made another interesting statement at a Soviet-Rumanian Friendship Meeting in Moscow on August 11. He declared that the Western powers want to "test our firmness," and that the issue of the peace treaty involves "a fight for the recognition of our grandeur." [7] Perhaps some of his listeners at the meeting recalled that less than two months earlier, when reporting on his talks with President Kennedy at Vienna, Khrushchev had deprecated alleged Western appeals "to questions of prestige." He had said that such appeals were "beneath criticism." [8]

The point is not that Khrushchev contradicted himself on the relevance of national grandeur in international affairs in applying a double standard to considerations of prestige. The point is rather that his invocation of Soviet "grandeur" at this juncture of the crisis may have been an attempt to evoke in Western statesmen, especially in De Gaulle, a sentiment he believed they would respect. But it is unlikely that either Khrushchev's remarks about the possible "strategic breakthrough" of Western policy or those referring to Soviet grandeur would have been made by a statesman who was fully confident that his cause would prevail. Moreover, from the Communist viewpoint, a statesman preoccupied with matters of prestige resembles the coward, the desperate suicide, and the reckless maniac: Like them, he has lost self-control, or is in danger of doing so, and jeopardizes the success of his cause by neglecting the facts that really matter. Perhaps it was in deference to Communist sobriety that Khrushchev's remarks on national grandeur were deleted in the Tass report of his statement; but by then the outburst had been duly noted in the West, and from the Communist viewpoint its effect may have justified this aberration from the norm of Bolshevist political propriety.

Khrushchev appeared to be on the defensive in yet

another respect. The Soviet notes to the three Western powers, dated August 3, revealed that the Soviet Government had become especially sensitive to the Western demand for self-determination by the Germans. The Soviet refusal to recognize this right is in flagrant conflict with the propaganda to which Moscow and Peking expose the developing countries in Asia and Africa. As usual, the Soviet Government tried to extricate itself from this dilemma by turning from the defensive to the offensive, but the effort was too frenzied to be convincing. The note to the U.S. Government spoke of "the manipulations with the slogan of self-determination" as "a rather cheap trick" and pointed out that "besides, it by no means benefits those in whose countries the social status, rights, and dignity of a man depend on the color of his skin and the bank account to teach democracy to the socialist states." [9] The note also mentioned that the U.S. Government maintained close contacts with such states as Spain, "where a fascist dictatorship, hated by the people . . . is reigning." [10] In one of the few passages in which the Soviet note to Paris deviated from that sent to Washington, the question was raised of why the French Government refused freedom to the people in Algeria and insisted on keeping the base at Bizerte.[11]

Similarly, large portions of Khrushchev's speech of August 7 were devoted to an attack on the "imperialists and colonialists" for their advocacy of self-determination, which, he said, they had disregarded in Vietnam, Algeria, Bizerte and Tunisia, the Congo, Angola, Cuba, Guatemala, and Taiwan. In addition, he accused Adenauer of hiding his plans of revenge behind the lofty slogan of self-determination.

But the continuing stream of refugees from the Soviet Zone seeking safety in West Berlin showed that words could no longer conceal or belittle the issue of self-determination. More than 30,000 refugees had left East Germany by the end of July; and from August 6 to August 8, West Berlin received 5,000 refugees, most of whom had held jobs in the Soviet Zone. The mass flight not only weakened the East German economy and undermined Ulbricht's political authority, but also had adverse effects on Soviet foreign policy in general.

In July and the first half of August, Ulbricht resorted to terror in a desperate effort to arrest the exodus. He intimidated those East Berliners who had to cross the border daily to go to work in West Berlin, and he imprisoned "agents" who were charged with inducing people to leave the Soviet Zone. Morale in the factories and on the collective farms deteriorated rapidly.[12]

On August 2, a West Berlin newspaper wrote: "It is incomprehensible why thus far the West has failed to reply to the numerous measures that Pankow has taken in violation of the rights of free movement throughout Berlin aimed at halting the stream of refugees." [13] Another newspaper pointed out that free movement in

Berlin concerns not only the Germans but also the Western allies, since this freedom was guaranteed by the four occupation powers.[14] At the meeting of the NATO council in Paris, Von Brentano informed the Western allies of Ulbricht's repressive measures.

Finally, during the night of August 12–13, the Ulbricht regime used police force and military detachments to close the boundary separating East from West Berlin. These illegal measures were taken under the pretext that it was necessary to prevent Western agents from entering the Soviet Zone and jeopardizing the security of the socialist states. In fact, Ulbricht hid behind the cloak of the Warsaw Pact countries, whose Communist leaders had proposed to him that he isolate West Berlin by closing the border. He published this recommendation along with his own decree.[15]

It is likely that Khrushchev authorized these measures not so much as the first of a series of unilateral actions against the Western powers but in order to weaken the position of the West in negotiations about the future status of Berlin and Germany. Ulbricht's repressive measures established a *fait accompli* in Khrushchev's favor, since the Western powers did not answer the Communist challenge by force to ensure the freedom of movement in the city as a whole. The four-power status of the city had been successfully undermined by the German Democratic Republic for many years; by the establishment of a state border within the city this status was now abolished *de facto*. The Western governments solemnly protested against the flagrant violation of the four-power status of the city and declared that they expected the Soviet Government "to put an end to these illegal measures." [16]

Khrushchev paid a price for his success. He demonstrated to the whole world Ulbricht's inability to govern the Soviet Zone without transforming it into a vast camp, sealed off from the West by military force. The Western powers tried to derive some propaganda advantage from this fact. But in the first days following the closing of the borders, they were dramatically reminded of an oft-forgotten premise of their policy: Their position in West Berlin is critically dependent on the morale of the West Berliners. If faith in the Western allies and their ability to defend self-determination were to falter, the Western position in West Berlin would, sooner or later, collapse. Morale in Berlin was badly shaken in the middle of August.

Immediately after the border was closed, Secretary Rusk issued a statement denouncing the Communist measure as a violation of the four-power agreement of June 20, 1949,[17] but his statement contained a sentence that claimed, with what a German observer termed a "sigh of relief," [18] that the position of the Western allies in West Berlin had not been affected by the closing of the border: "Available information indicates that measures taken thus far are aimed at residents of East Berlin and East Germany and not at the Western position in West Berlin or access thereto." [19]

The West Berliners were disappointed and angry. The trade unions expressed their disillusionment over the passivity of the West. At a mass rally in front of West Berlin's City Hall, posters were displayed expressing the disenchantment of the population and demanding Western action rather than mere words of protest. Mayor Brandt announced that he had sent a letter to President Kennedy suggesting that action be taken against the Communists. The German Ambassador to the United States admitted in Washington that there existed a feeling of disappointment in West Germany over the Allied reaction to the new Communist measures in Berlin.

A few days later, when it appeared that the acute danger of a clash between Ulbricht's police and the infuriated West Berliners had passed, the Soviet Ambassador in Bonn assured Adenauer that no unilateral steps would be taken by Khrushchev, so that nothing untoward would happen prior to the German election on September 17, 1961.

A week after the closing of the border, the U.S. Government reinforced its garrison in West Berlin by 1,500 men. This force came to the city via the military road through the Soviet Zone. The Communists did not interfere with their progress toward Berlin, just as the Western powers had not interfered with the armed isolation of West Berlin. In addition, Vice-President Lyndon Johnson visited Bonn and Berlin to assure the Germans in ringing tones of continued Western support. Both the American troops and the Vice-President were cheered; morale in West Berlin was boosted.

Thus, there has been some counteraction, at least locally. The question remains, however, whether on balance it is Communism or the free West that benefited more from the events of August, 1961. The United States had reasserted, by action taken with the support of Great Britain and France, that it would not surrender the West's rights of presence in West Berlin and of access to the city. They put Communist respect for these rights to a test. The Western powers were successful, for the time being, in reaffirming the *status quo* in *West* Berlin. By contrast, the Communists had taken some probing action in the city that affected the position and policy of the Western allies adversely, at least in the short run, and they have succeeded in changing the *status quo* of divided Berlin by defying the West.

August 21, 1961

Notes

CHAPTER 1

1. See Theodor Eschenburg, *Die deutsche Frage*, R. Oldenbourg, Munich, 1959.
2. See Philip E. Mosely, "The Occupation of Germany: New Light on How the Zones Were Drawn," in *The Kremlin and World Politics*, New York, 1960, pp. 155–58.
3. See W. Phillips Davison, *The Berlin Blockade*, Princeton University Press, Princeton, N. J., 1957.
4. According to Ernst Lemmer, Minister of All-German Affairs in the Federal Republic, West Berlin security authorities investigated 265 successful abductions from West Berlin in the period from the end of the war to May 31, 1961. *Der Tagesspiegel* (Berlin), July 9, 1961.
5. Press and Information Office of the Federal Republic, *Bulletin*, February 17, 1961. Twenty-five per cent of the total of 2.5 million are displaced persons who fled first to the Soviet Zone or to East Berlin.
6. For a vivid description, see "Der Stacheldraht der DDR," *Neue Zürcher Zeitung* (Zurich), October 1, 1960.
7. *The New York Times*, July 26, 1961.

Notes

CHAPTER 2

1. For the text of the Soviet note, see *The New York Times,* November 28, 1958. For a critical discussion of the omissions and distortions of historical facts to be found in this note, see Department of State, *The Soviet Note on Berlin: An Analysis,* Department of State Publication 6757, January, 1959 (hereafter cited as *The Soviet Note on Berlin*).
2. *The New York Times,* November 29, 1958. I am indebted to Arnold Horelick for the information that these remarks were not reported in Soviet media.
3. The *intermediate* demands, in turn, may be said to have comprised various agreements differing with regard to their terms, including the date on which the agreement would be implemented.
4. For the use of this tactic in the Suez crisis, see Hans Speier, "Soviet Atomic Blackmail and the North Atlantic Alliance," *World Politics,* April, 1957.
5. Gerhard Lindner, "Zur Lufthoheit der DDR," *Deutsche Aussenpolitik,* October, 1957, pp. 830 ff.

CHAPTER 3

1. See the four-power communiqué of December 14, 1958, and the NATO declaration on Berlin of December 16, 1958.
2. U.S. note of December 31, 1958. The British and French notes of the same date used similar expressions. The term "ultimatum" occurred in all three notes.
3. See Foreign Minister V.M. Molotov's speech of November 8, 1955, at the Geneva Conference of Foreign Ministers and Foreign Minister Heinrich von Brentano's analysis of the Soviet position in his speech to the German Bundestag, December 1, 1955. The Communist position can be traced back to November, 1950, when Otto Grotewohl, Premier of the East German Government, proposed to the Bonn Government the establishment of an "All German Constituent Council," which was explained in detail by Ulbricht in his speech of January 17, 1959.
4. *Frankfurter Allgemeine Zeitung,* March 31, 1959.
5. See Khrushchev's election speech of February 24, 1959; the Soviet notes to the United States, Britain, and France of March 2, 1959;

and many similar utterances by Khrushchev and other Soviet leaders since then.
6. *Le Monde* (Paris), March 27, 1959.
7. *The Current Digest of the Soviet Press*, March 2, 1960, p. 15. For an official West German view of the Oder-Neisse Line, see Franz Thedieck, "Die Oder-Neisse-Linie ein europäisches Problem," in Presse-und Informationsamt der Bundesregierung, *Bulletin*, November 24, 1959. A brief historical account of the issue is presented by H. Siegler, in *Wiedervereinigung und Sicherheit Deutschlands*, 3rd edition, November, 1958, pp. 15 ff. For a discussion of former High Commissioner John J. McCloy's well-known 1956 proposal on the issue, see Hans Speier, *German Rearmament and Atomic War*, Row, Peterson and Company, Evanston, Ill., 1957, pp. 240 ff.

CHAPTER 4

1. See Khrushchev's speeches of June 15 and July 8, 1961.
2. *The New York Times*, June 13, 1959. On "abnormality," see also the U.S. note of December 31, 1958 (*The Soviet Note on Berlin*, p. 35), and President Eisenhower's press conferences of September 28, 1959, and February 17, 1960. Unfortunately, in the President's statements, the relation between "abnormality" and the failure of reunification was not made explicit. Another correct description of the abnormality of the situation in Berlin and Germany was contained in the speech on April 30, 1960, by the then Under Secretary of State, Douglas Dillon; in Department of State *Bulletin*, May 9, 1960, p. 725.
3. In Berlin, November 28, 1959 (mimeographed text issued November 30, 1959, by Presse- und Informationsamt des Landes Berlin, Nr. 278).
4. *The New York Times*, November 28, 1958.
5. *The Current Digest of the Soviet Press*, March 2, 1960, p. 15.

CHAPTER 5

1. Averell Harriman, "My Alarming Interview with Khrushchev," *Life*, July 8, 1959. See also Joseph Alsop's column on Mr. Harri-

man's interview, "Method in Khrushchev's Madness," *The Washington Post*, July 20, 1959.

2. *The New York Times*, January 15, 1960.

CHAPTER 6

1. *The Soviet Note on Berlin*, p. 32.
2. Joachim Rottmann, *Der Viermächte-Status Berlins*, issued by the Ministry of All-German Affairs, Deutscher Bundes-Verlag, Bonn, 1959, p. 12.
3. Speech at Douglas, Georgia; in Department of State *Bulletin*, April 24, 1961, p. 589.
4. A neutral observer stationed in Berlin, who is well informed about developments in East Germany, told the author in December, 1959, that these efforts have been quite successful: Many non-Communist East Germans believe that the Western powers in fact "negotiated" with East Germany at Geneva. In the light of the political advantages reaped by the East German Government at Geneva, Adenauer's decision not to attend the forthcoming summit meeting in order not to facilitate Ulbricht's attendance appears to have been eminently sound.
5. *The New York Times*, June 13, 1959; see also *Neue Zürcher Zeitung*, June 14, 1959.
6. Khrushchev's speech to the Hungarian Party Congress, December 1, 1959, in *The Current Digest of the Soviet Press*, December 20, 1959, p. 7.
7. He used the same words in his speech of January 14, 1960.
8. Khrushchev took issue with a suggestion Adenauer had made in one of his speeches that instead of "reunification" the Germans should make use of the expression "the return of freedom to 17 million Germans." After citing this statement, Khrushchev exclaimed, "Unilateral solutions are possible only through war, while disputes are resolved by negotiation only if mutual interests are taken into consideration. But where is the consideration of interests here when it is demanded as an ultimatum that the socialist achievements of the first workers' and peasants' state in the history of Germany be done away with, that the German Democratic Republic be done away with?" Speech of January 14, 1960.
9. Letters to that effect were sent to President Eisenhower on December 10, 1957; February 1, 1958; and March 6, 1958.

10. See the editorial, "Ein Jahr danach," *Der Tagesspiegel,* November 29, 1959.

CHAPTER 7

1. ". . . the Soviet Government is ready to open negotiations with the Governments of the United States and other countries concerned on granting West Berlin the status of a demilitarized Free City. If this proposal is not acceptable to the United States Government, there is no topic left for talks on the Berlin question by the former occupying powers." Soviet note of November 27, 1958.
2. *The New York Times,* November 28, 1958.
3. Press Department of the Embassy of the U.S.S.R., Release No. 154, Washington, D.C., March 28, 1960.
4. These warnings were first made by President Eisenhower in his address on "Atoms for Peace and Progress" before the General Assembly of the United Nations on December 8, 1953, and again at his press conference on March 16, 1955. See Speier, *German Rearmament and Atomic War,* p. 101.
5. The earlier Soviet arguments against Western views of limited war are summarized in Bulganin's letter to President Eisenhower, dated December 10, 1957. See *The New York Times,* December 12, 1957. The impossibility of limiting war in Europe was advanced by Colonel Vasilyev, who wrote in December, 1957, that "any small war in Europe would automatically lead to a world war."
6. Speech of January 14, 1960.
7. *Ibid.*

CHAPTER 8

1. Press conference of March 19, 1959.
2. See, for example, "Mr. Khrushchev's Vanishing Act," *The Economist,* March 28, 1959.
3. The bargaining value of West German disarmament was dismissed by Khrushchev himself at his press conference on November 27, 1958. He was asked by the Reuters correpondent V. Buist, "Will there be any change in the Soviet government's policy on Berlin should Western Germany give up her rearmament programme?" Khrushchev replied, "One cannot regard Western Germany's re-

Notes

nunciation of her rearmament programme as being a concession for a concession. These are two different things and of different value. Should Western Germany declare that she will not arm herself, with the occupation regime of Berlin still maintained, the source of tension and conflict will not be stamped out. It will remain." *Soviet News* (published by the Press Department of the Soviet Embassy in London), November 28, 1958, p. 191.
4. F. R. Allemann, "Was will der Westen?" *Der Monat*, May, 1959, p. 10.
5. Khrushchev commented on this Western idea in June, 1959, in a speech at the Kremlin welcoming the delegation of the Central Committee of the Socialist Unity Party of Germany on their return to Moscow from a trip through the Soviet Union. He said, "This reasoning is naive to say the least. It is plain to all that the Western powers wish thereby to degrade the German Democratic Republic and are trying in the bargain to do so through the agency of the Soviet Union. These gentlemen evidently suffer from the absence of a sense of reality, showing a disrespect for the Soviet Union as a partner in the war against Hitlerite Germany." *The Current Digest of the Soviet Press*, July 26, 1959, p. 12.
6. *Neue Zürcher Zeitung*, July 31, 1959.
7. A. A. Gromyko at the first plenary session on June 19, 1959.
8. Harriman, *op. cit.*

CHAPTER 9

1. For the next six months, the old threat was repeated explicitly on only a few occasions—especially in addressing Communist audiences or the Federal Republic.
2. The threat of a separate peace treaty with East Germany was repeated in Khrushchev's speeches at Budapest on December 1, 1959, and at Moscow on January 14, 1960, as well as at his press conference at Jakarta (printed in *Izvestia* on March 1, 1960). See *The Current Digest of the Soviet Press*, March 30, 1960, p. 6. At that press conference, Khrushchev said quite pointedly, "When a peace treaty has been signed with the German Democratic Republic, all the consequences deriving from the war against Germany will cease to exist, as concerns West Berlin as well."
3. Press conference in Washington, D.C., September 27, 1959; reproduced in *Let Us Live in Peace and Friendship: The Visit of N. S. Khrushchev to the U.S.A.*, Moscow, 1959, p. 337.

4. Speech in Washington, D.C., on October 1, 1959; in Department of State *Bulletin*, October 19, 1959, p. 545.

5. The visit was officially set to take place from June 10 to 19, that is, after the summit meeting in Paris.

6. When Adenauer visited the United States in March, 1960, Soviet propaganda used these statements to create the impression that the President and the Chancellor were in disagreement.

7. The substitution in the Budapest speech was cited by F. R. Allemann, in "Germany Fears a Berlin Deal," *The New Leader*, January 11, 1960, p. 11. It should be noted, however, that in Budapest, Khrushchev still spoke of Soviet interest in "abolishing *the seat* of the occupation regime." Frol R. Kozlov, at the end of his visit to the United States, had said on this subject, "we proposed an end to the unjustifiably protracted occupation regime and a free-city status for West Berlin." *The New York Times*, July 12, 1959.

8. "On Peaceful Coexistence," *Foreign Affairs*, October, 1959, pp. 10 and 13.

9. On November 25, 1959, *Neues Deutschland*, the central organ of the Communist press in East Germany, carried three large banner headlines: "Five Million Americans Heard the Truth about the D.D.R. [German Democratic Republic]"; "Walter Ulbricht Spoke on U.S.A.-Television"; "Summit Meeting Will Prepare Peace Treaty."

10. *Ibid.*

11. Speech of January 14, 1960.

12. December 12, 1959.

13. Khrushchev's "On Peaceful Coexistence," *op. cit.*, p. 14

14. *The Current Digest of the Soviet Press*, December 30, 1959, p. 48.

15. *The New York Times*, April 7, 1960. It must be recognized, however, that Adenauer provided the Communists with some arguments for their campaign against Bonn, especially by his stubborn reluctance for a very long time to part with Theodor Oberländer, a high official under the Nazis, as a member of his cabinet.

16. December 1, 1959.

17. Headline in *Neues Deutschland*, November 14, 1959.

18. *Frankfurter Allgemeine Zeitung*, January 16, 1960.

19. *Der Kurier* (Berlin), December 22, 1959.

20. *Der Tag* (Berlin), December 24, 1959.

21. See Willy Brandt's speech in the foreign-policy debate of the German Bundestag on November 5, 1959 (*Bundestag Record*, pp. 4725–27).

Notes

CHAPTER 10

1. *Dokumente zur Berlin-Frage 1944–1959*, edited by Forschungsinstitut der deutschen Gesellschaft für Auswärtige Politik in collaboration with the Senate of Berlin, R. Oldenbourg, Munich, 1959, p. 133. This book is the most complete collection of all relevant documents. For the corresponding letter of the Allied Kommandatura of May 14, 1949, see *ibid.*, p. 122.
2. *Ibid.*, p. 120.
3. *Ibid.*, p. 162.
4. The Law on the Federal Constitutional Court (Bundesverfassungsgerichtsgesetz) of March 12, 1951, and its revision of July 21, 1956, were vetoed. Similarly, in July, 1960, a Federal law prohibiting the distribution of Communist propaganda was vetoed. *The New York Times* of August 1, 1960, commented that the application of this law in Berlin was vetoed in order "not to give the Soviet Union any pretext for unilateral steps against West Berlin." Several other laws, especially those pertaining to defense, do not apply to Berlin.
5. This Declaration of the Allied Kommandatura of May 5, 1955 (*Dokumente zur Berlin-Frage 1944–1959*, pp. 241-44), is still in force.
6. Article VI of the Convention on Relations between the Three Powers and the Federal Republic of October 23, 1954. *Ibid.*, p. 226.
7. See the figures from 1956 to 1959 and their breakdown in Bruce L. R. Smith, "The Governance of Berlin," *International Conciliation*, November, 1959, p. 207.
8. The figures are from *Die Berliner Wirtschaft*, January 2, 1959, as quoted by Bruce L. R. Smith, *op. cit.*, p. 209.
9. These figures were mentioned by Chancellor Adenauer in his speech at Berlin on January 11, 1960. See *Der Tagesspiegel*, January 12, 1960.
10. See especially Martin Drath, "Berlin und Bonn—Die Rechtsstellung Berlins in der Bundesrepublik Deutschland," *Juristische Rundschau*, 1951, pp. 385 ff.
11. See Heinz Kreutzer, "Das Öffentliche Recht in Berlin—Die besondere staatsrechtliche Situation und die Rechtsentwicklung von 1945 bis 1954," *Die Öffentliche Verwaltung*, Sonderdruck from Issues 1, 2, 3, and 5, 1955. For further studies by Drath and Kreutzer, see Rottmann, *op. cit.*, p. 45, n. 91.

12. The Five Point Declaration was distributed (in mimeographed form) by the Presse- und Informationsamt des Landes Berlin only on February 16, 1960.
13. *The Current Digest of the Soviet Press,* March 30, 1960, p. 6.
14. Professor Tunkin's article appeared in *Izvestia* on February 18, 1960. For further West German comment, see the article by Johannes Gross in *Deutsche Zeitung,* February 13–14, 1960; *Die Welt,* February 19 and March 3, 1960; and *Süddeutsche Zeitung,* February 19, 1960.
15. *The New York Times,* March 25, 1960.

CHAPTER 11

1. *Der Tagesspiegel,* January 12, 1960.
2. *Ibid.*
3. *Der Tag,* January 12, 1960.
4. January 28, 1960.
5. According to a report by Drew Middleton in *The New York Times,* January 13, 1960, the liberal *News Chronicle* regarded Adenauer's speech as a direct provocation of Prime Minister Macmillan.
6. "Unhappy Allies," *The New Leader,* April 11, 1960, p. 3.
7. F. R. Allemann, "Germany under Attack," *The New Leader,* April 11, 1960, p. 6.
8. For example, *Die Welt* pointed out on January 12, 1960, that Adenauer's arguments would be impressive if London and Washington, too, were ready to forget about the Geneva proposals. "But that the Allies do not do. Immediately after the conclusion of the Western summit conference in Paris, one of the most highly placed Americans declared last December, 'We would be glad if the Soviets accepted our last offer [of July 28, 1959] for an interim solution.' This is not unknown to the Russians." On January 20, 1960, *Der Spiegel* gleefully reported foreign criticism of Adenauer's speech.
9. See Helmut Schmidt, *Verteidigung oder Vergeltung,* Stuttgart, 1961.
10. *Der Tag,* February 17, 1960.
11. *Neue Zürcher Zeitung,* February 7, 1960.
12. Lack of political sophistication and vigilance in dealing with Communists is not confined to certain American businessmen. At

Notes

the 1960 Spring Fair in Leipzig, the presence of some Ruhr industrialists and their talks with Ulbricht and other high-ranking East German politicians were cited in the German Communist press as proof that "an understanding between the German Democratic Republic and the Federal Republic was possible" (*Neues Deutschland,* March 8, 1960). A West German paper reported that Communist propaganda "tried to present the world-wide recognition of the two German states as an established fact, which was accepted by business and still sabotaged only by Bonn" (*Christ und Welt,* March 3, 1960). Both Adenauer and the President of the Federal Association of German Industry publicly condemned the conduct of these West German industrialists (*Der Tagesspiegel,* March 12, 1960). It should be noted that the Ruhr industry is interested in steel exports. Only 4 per cent of the total West German exports, but more than 20 per cent of the exports of the West German steel industry, go to Eastern-bloc countries.

13. Richard Lowenthal, "Die Euphorie des Westens," *Der Monat,* February, 1960, p. 14.
14. Especially Secretary Herter on November 24, 1959.
15. *Die Welt,* March 23, 1960.
16. *Süddeutsche Zeitung,* March 13, 1960. The paper attributed this story to Washington observers.
17. See *Die Welt,* March 19, 1960. See also *Vorwärts,* March 25, 1960.
18. *Der Tagesspiegel,* March 18, 1960, asked, "Was the plan of a plebiscite the reaction to the talk with Eisenhower or its result?" For similar comment, see *Der Tag,* March 18, 1960.
19. *Der Tag,* March 22, 1960.
20. *Deutsche Zeitung,* March 19, 1960.
21. *Der Telegraf,* March 25, 1960.
22. *Der Zeit,* March 25, 1960.
23. *The New York Times,* January 17, 1960.
24. *Ibid.,* February 9, 1960.
25. *Ibid.*
26. *Ibid.*
27. *Die Welt,* March 23, 1960.
28. Tass, April 3, 1960.
29. At a press conference on April 8, 1960, Secretary Herter said that he had no specific information on these reports. See Department of State *Bulletin,* April 25, 1960, p. 643.
30. *Frankfurter Allgemeine Zeitung,* February 20 and 23, 1960.
31. *Neue Zürcher Zeitung,* February 23, 1960.

32. William J. Jordan, *The New York Times,* March 10, 1960. This issue of the *Times* also contains Eisenhower's ruling and Herter's press conference, at which he explained its rationale.
33. For example, Richard Lowenthal wrote that the West was in a position of confusion, disillusion, and disunity, "which is without precedent in the past twenty years." *Loc. cit.*
34. *The New York Times,* April 3, 1960. In the same dispatch by Arthur J. Olsen, British military authorities were reported to have disagreed on the basis of "political, not military, considerations" with the American officers on this issue.
35. The idea of a plebiscite had already been rejected by Khrushchev in his press conference at Jakarta on February 29, 1960, in reaction to press reports about a "Herter Plan" on plebiscites to be proposed at the Paris summit meeting.
36. Department of State *Bulletin,* April 25, 1960, p. 638. In his press conference on April 8, 1960, Herter re-emphasized this point. *Ibid.,* p. 643.
37. Department of State *Bulletin,* March 9, 1960, pp. 754 ff.
38. Speech at Baku on April 25, 1960; see *The New York Times,* April 26, 1960.

CHAPTER 12

1. Department of State *Bulletin,* March 30, 1960, p. 851.
2. Speech of May 20, 1960; in Department of State *Bulletin,* June 6, 1960, p. 900.
3. After his return from Paris, Eisenhower said on May 20, 1960, "The usefulness of this work has been well established through four years of effort. The Soviets were not aware of it. . . . These flights have given us information of the greatest importance to the nation's security. In fact, their success has been nothing short of remarkable." *Ibid.*
4. Department of State *Bulletin,* May 20, 1960, p. 852.
5. See Philip E. Mosely, "Soviet Myth and Reality," *Foreign Affairs,* April, 1961, pp. 341–44.
6. May 20, 1960; in Department of State *Bulletin,* p. 901.
7. *The Current Digest of the Soviet Press,* June 22, 1960.
8. He said about the Mayor, "I don't know where he was during the war, whether he was at the front or whether he realizes what it smells of." *Ibid.*
9. *Ibid.*

Notes

10. *Ibid.*
11. *Ibid.*
12. *The New York Times*, May 17, 1960.
13. The following quotations of Khrushchev's remarks are from *The Current Digest of the Soviet Press*, June 15, 1960, p. 10.
14. For an analysis of the meaning of "provocation" in Bolshevik parlance, see Nathan Leites, *A Study of Bolshevism*, The Free Press, Glencoe, Ill., 1953, pp. 321–23.
15. The following quotations are from *The New York Times*, October 8, 1960. The *Times* reported that the interest aroused by Khrushchev's statement on Berlin was overshadowed by the question whether Macmillan had really given Khrushchev the assurance about the summit meeting. On October 7, a spokesman for Macmillan denied that "such positive assurance" had been given.
16. After the Paris meeting, he made such threats in Moscow on June 3, in Austria on July 1, 4, and 8, in a letter to Macmillan on August 4, and in his report on the Moscow Conference on January 6, 1961. It should be noted that the specific threat to Western rights of access to Berlin occurred only twice in this period, at the press conference in Moscow on June 3 and in Vienna on July 8.

CHAPTER 13

1. A resolution proclaiming Berlin the capital of Germany after reunification was passed by the Bundestag on February 6, 1957.
2. *Frankfurter Allgemeine Zeitung*, July 9, 1960.
3. "Chruschtschows neue Berlin-Drohung," Presse- und Informationsamt der Bundesregierung, *Bulletin*, July 15, 1960.
4. *The New York Times*, July 21, 1960.
5. In a television interview; see *Neues Deutschland*, September 4, 1960.
6. ADN [Communist news agency], August 30, 1960.
7. *The Times* (London), September 1, 1960.
8. *The Washington Post*, September 1, 1960.
9. *L'Aurore* (Paris), September 1, 1960.
10. *The Daily Telegraph* (London) of August 29, 1960, commented, "There must be persons in Bonn old enough to recall why week-end speeches in Germany about the frontier with Poland revive in Britain the most painful memories." *The Times* inter-

preted Erhard's speech to mean that the Federal Government
would not be content "until the old Bismarckian Germany has
been put together again."
11. ADN, September 8, 1960.
12. ADN, September 13, 1960.
13. ADN, September 27, 1960.
14. *Neues Deutschland,* September 4, 1960.
15. *Frankfurter Allgemeine Zeitung,* July 16, 1960.

CHAPTER 14

1. "The President," *Foreign Affairs,* April, 1960, p. 361.
2. *Ibid.,* p. 367.
3. Speech to the World Affairs Council in Boston on December 1,
   1959. See Wilhelm Grewe, "Ueber die 'Gipfel'–Diplomatie," *Neue
   Zürcher Zeitung,* January 12, 1960.
4. Press conference of January 25, 1961; see *The New York Times,*
   January 26, 1961.
5. *The New York Times,* January 28, 1961.
6. *Ibid.*
7. Agreement that the reply should no longer be postponed was
   reached by the foreign ministers of the United States, Great
   Britain, France, and West Germany as late as May, 1961, at the
   Oslo meeting of the NATO council. The German reply was
   presented on July 12.
8. *The Current Digest of the Soviet Press,* March 29, 1961, p. 21.
9. *Ibid.,* p. 20.
10. The text of the Soviet *aide-mémoire* of June 4, 1961, was published
    by *The New York Times* on June 12, 1961. Curiously enough, it
    was first released by the Soviet Government in German, perhaps
    in order to counteract any initial optimistic interpretations in
    Germany of the results of the Vienna meeting.
11. Any four-power negotiations to urge the Federal Government and
    the Ulbricht regime to negotiate would require an indefinite
    amount of time prior to the beginning of the six-month period in
    which the Germans would try to reach a preliminary agreement.
    Thereafter, further time would be required for four-power negotia-
    tions. For all these reasons, the *aide-mémoire* did not contain "an
    ultimatum."
12. *The New York Times,* July 16, 1961.
13. *Ibid.,* July 19, 1961.

Notes

14. *Ibid.*, June 12, 1961.
15. *Ibid.*, June 16, 1961.
16. *Ibid.*
17. Speech at a Kremlin meeting of the Soviet-Vietnamese Friendship Society on June 28, 1961.
18. Speech at Moscow on July 8, 1961.
19. *Ibid.*
20. *Ibid.*
21. Speech of June 28, 1961.
22. Speech of July 8, 1961.
23. Speech of June 28, 1961.
24. *Aide-mémoire* of June 4, 1961; in *The New York Times,* June 12, 1961.
25. Speech of July 8, 1961.
26. Television report of June 15 on the meeting at Vienna and speech of June 28, 1961.
27. Speech of June 28, 1961.
28. *Ibid.*
29. Speech of July 8, 1961.
30. This Soviet *aide-mémoire* was also prepared for the Vienna meeting. See *The New York Times,* June 12, 1960.
31. Wilfried Hertz-Eichenrode, "Die Salami-Taktik," *Deutsche Zeitung* (Stuttgart), June 28, 1961.

CHAPTER 15

1. The quotations in this chapter from the U.S. note of July 17 are taken from *The New York Times,* July 19, 1961.
2. In his speech on July 25, the President said that "if anyone doubts the legality of our rights in Berlin, we are ready to have it submitted to adjudication." *The New York Times,* July 26, 1961.
3. House of Commons, Parliamentary Debates; in *Weekly Hansard,* No. 523, p. 1386.
4. *The New York Times,* July 24, 1961.
5. *Ibid.*
6. *Ibid.*, July 26, 1961.
7. *Ibid.*
8. See Rainer Hildebrandt, "Ulbricht's Wettlauf mit der Zeit," *Der Tagesspiegel,* July 2, 1961; Rene Bayer, "Die Versorgungskrise in der Zone," *Süddeutsche Zeitung,* July 1, 1961.

9. *Neue Zürcher Zeitung,* July 18, 1961. The figures cited in this paragraph are taken from the article by Otto Frei.
10. *Ibid.* On the flight of students from the Soviet Zone, see also *Der Tagesspiegel,* July 2, 1961.
11. This sample of disaffection is taken from a report in the West Berlin newspaper *Morgenpost,* July 7, 1961.
12. *Frankfurter Allgemeine Zeitung,* July 8, 1961.
13. Reported in American newspapers on the basis of accounts that appeared in the West Berlin *Telegraf,* July 23, 1961.

CHAPTER 16

1. Speech of July 25, 1961; see *The New York Times,* July 26, 1961.
2. *Ibid.*
3. *Ibid.*
4. The text of this declaration was published on July 1, 1961, in *Die Welt, Deutsche Zeitung, Der Tag,* and many other West German newspapers. Gerstenmaier is a member of the Christian Democratic Union, the government party, but his declaration was greeted with special enthusiasm by the political opposition. It was reported that Adenauer himself warned against "a too intensive interpretation" of Gerstenmaier's declaration.

   See *Süddeutsche Zeitung,* July 4, 1961; *Telegraf,* July 5, 1961; and *Rheinischer Merkur,* July 7, 1961. *Rheinischer Merkur* of July 7, 1961, wrote that Gerstenmaier's "coup" was based on co-operation with the Social Democratic leader Herbert Wehner, and that the parliamentary committee on foreign affairs, the West German Foreign Office, the Federal Government, and the Chancellor had not been "sufficiently informed" in advance of Gerstenmaier's initiative.

POSTSCRIPT

1. *Neue Zürcher Zeitung,* August 1, 1961. Khrushchev made a similar statement at a Soviet-Rumanian Friendship Meeting in the Kremlin on August 11, 1961; see *The New York Times,* August 12, 1961.
2. *Neue Zürcher Zeitung,* August 1, 1961.
3. Khrushchev's speech was broadcast by Tass in English to Europe on August 7, 1961.
4. *The New York Times,* August 4 and 12, 1961.

Notes

5. Tass broadcast, August 7, 1961.
6. *Ibid.*
7. *The New York Times,* August 12, 1961.
8. Khrushchev's radio-television report of June 15; see *The New York Times,* June 16, 1961.
9. *The New York Times,* August 5, 1961.
10. *Ibid.*
11. *Neue Zürcher Zeitung,* August 6, 1961.
12. See the articles by O[tto] F[rei] in *Neue Zürcher Zeitung,* August 4 and 12, 1961. See also the article by Harry Gilroy in *The New York Times,* August 13, 1961.
13. *Der Tagesspiegel,* August 2, as cited in *Neue Zürcher Zeitung,* August 4, 1961.
14. *Morgenpost,* August 2, as cited in *Neue Zürcher Zeitung,* August 4, 1961.
15. For the text of these documents, see *The New York Times,* August 14, 1961.
16. For the text of the U.S. note of August 17, 1961, see *The New York Times,* August 18, 1961.
17. *The New York Times,* August 14, 1961.
18. Sebastian Haffner, in *Die Welt,* August 15, 1961.
19. *The New York Times,* August 14, 1961. On August 15, the Western commandants as well sent a protest to the Soviet commandant. See *The New York Times,* August 16, 1961. The Soviet reply was unresponsive and condescending in tone.

Other Volumes
of RAND Research

THE UNIVERSITY OF CHICAGO PRESS
CHICAGO, ILLINOIS

Water Supply: Economics, Technology, and Policy, by
Jack Hirshleifer, James C. DeHaven, and Jerome W.
Milliman, 1960

COLUMBIA UNIVERSITY PRESS
NEW YORK, NEW YORK

Soviet National Income and Product, 1940–48, by Abram
Bergson and Hans Heymann, Jr., 1954
Soviet National Income and Product in 1928, by Oleg
Hoeffding, 1954
Labor Productivity in Soviet and American Industry, by
Walter Galenson, 1955

Other Volumes of RAND Research

THE FREE PRESS, GLENCOE, ILLINOIS

Psychosis and Civilization, by Herbert Goldhamer and
Andrew W. Marshall, 1953
Soviet Military Doctrine, by Raymond L. Garthoff, 1953
À Study of Bolshevism, by Nathan Leites, 1953
Ritual of Liquidation: The Case of the Moscow Trials,
by Nathan Leites and Elsa Bernaut, 1954
*Two Studies in Soviet Controls: Communism and the
Russian Peasant, and Moscow in Crisis,* by Herbert S.
Dinerstein and Leon Gouré, 1955
A Million Random Digits with 100,000 Normal Deviates,
by The RAND Corporation, 1955

HARVARD UNIVERSITY PRESS
CAMBRIDGE, MASSACHUSETTS

Smolensk under Soviet Rule, by Merle Fainsod, 1958
The Economics of Defense in the Nuclear Age, by Charles
J. Hitch and Roland McKean, 1960

THE MACMILLAN COMPANY
NEW YORK, NEW YORK

*China Crosses the Yalu: The Decision To Enter the Korean
War,* by Allen S. Whiting, 1960
Protective Construction in a Nuclear Age, edited by J. J.
O'Sullivan, 1961
The Determination of Orbits, by A. D. Dubyago; trans-
lated from the Russian by R. D. Burke, G. Gordon,
L. N. Rowell, and F. T. Smith, 1961

Other Volumes of RAND Research

NORTH-HOLLAND PUBLISHING COMPANY,
AMSTERDAM, HOLLAND

A Time Series Analysis of Interindustry Demands, by
Kenneth J. Arrow and Marvin Hoffenberg, 1959

FREDERICK A. PRAEGER, INC.
NEW YORK, NEW YORK

*War and the Soviet Union: Nuclear Weapons and the
Revolution in Soviet Military and Political Thinking,*
by H. S. Dinerstein, 1959

PRINCETON UNIVERSITY PRESS,
PRINCETON, NEW JERSEY

Approximations for Digital Computers, by Cecil Hastings,
Jr., 1955
*International Communication and Political Opinion: A
Guide to the Literature,* by Bruce Lannes Smith and
Chitra M. Smith, 1956
Dynamic Programming, by Richard Bellman, 1957
The Berlin Blockade: A Study in Cold War Politics, by
W. Phillips Davison, 1958
The French Economy and the State, by Warren C. Baum,
1958
Strategy in the Missile Age, by Bernard Brodie, 1959
Foreign Aid: Theory and Practice in Southern Asia, by
Charles Wolf, Jr., 1960
Adaptive Control Processes: A Guided Tour, by Richard
Bellman, 1961

Other Volumes of RAND Research

STANFORD UNIVERSITY PRESS
STANFORD, CALIFORNIA

Strategic Surrender: The Politics of Victory and Defeat,
by Paul Kecskemeti, 1958

On the Game of Politics in France, by Nathan Leites, 1959

Atomic Energy in the Soviet Union, by Arnold Kramish,
1959

Marxism in Southeast Asia: A Study of Four Countries,
edited by Frank N. Trager, 1959

JOHN WILEY & SONS, INC.
NEW YORK, NEW YORK

*Efficiency in Government through Systems Analysis: With
Emphasis on Water Resource Development,* by Roland
N. McKean, 1958